Latter-day Saint Heroes & Heroines

VOLUME TWO

Marlene Bateman Sullivan

Distributed by:

GRANITE
PUBLISHING & DISTRIBUTION L.L.C.

Granite Publishing and Distribution, LLC
868 North 1430 West
Orem, Utah 84057
(801) 229-9023 • Toll Free (800) 574-5779
Fax (801) 229-1924

Page Layout & Design by Myrna Varga, The Office Connection, Inc.
Cover Design by Tammie Ingram

The Chosen Seer and the Well Beloved Brother
©Robert T. Barrett
used by permission

Library of Congress Control Number: 2003107557
ISBN: 1-932280-09-X

Printed in the United States of America
Second Printing September 2003
10 9 8 7 6 5 4 3 2

To Kelly, *my* hero

Contents

Chapter 1

Dennison Harris & Robert Scott

FOILING THE PLOT AGAINST THE PROPHET

Joseph Smith had faced intense persecution ever since revealing that he had seen Heavenly Father and Jesus Christ in a vision, yet never before had his life been in such peril as it was in 1844. That spring, the Prophet was dismayed to learn that some of his most dangerous enemies were those who stood by his side, leading the Church. Fortunately, Joseph had two loyal young men, Dennison L. Harris and Robert Scott, on his side and it was these two boys who bravely risked their lives to foil a deadly plot against the prophet.

The story begins late one afternoon. Dennison, a young man of seventeen, was sitting on the woodpile in front of his house, feeling worried and perplexed. He glanced up to see his good friend, Robert Scott, walking down the road toward him.

Dennison invited him to sit down, but after chatting casually a few minutes, a strange silence fell between the two comrades. Dennison noticed that his friend was looking rather glum and asked what was troubling him. Robert hesitated, then remarked on Dennison's own somber countenance. With some surprise, each discovered that the other was feeling anxious about some private problem. Being great friends, they agreed to exchange secrets, promising each other that the information would go no further than the wood they sat upon.

Dennison went first and explained that he had been invited by Austin A. Cowles to attend a secret meeting. Cowles, currently a member of the High Council, was one of the leaders of a secret movement whose aim was to have Joseph Smith declared a fallen prophet. When Cowles invited Dennison to come to the meeting, he asked the boy to invite his father but cautioned him not to breathe a word to anyone else.

With some consternation, Robert admitted that he too had been invited to the clandestine meeting, but by another man, William Law. Robert loved and respected Joseph Smith but felt a certain loyalty to Law since he had given Robert a home and had raised him as a member of his own family. Law, who was Joseph's first counselor in the First Presidency of the Church, had lately become harshly critical of the Prophet. However, he only voiced his complaints when Joseph was not around.

"Well, Den," Robert asked finally. "Are you going to attend the meeting?"

"I don't know, are you?"

"I don't know whether to go or not," Robert hedged. "Suppose we go in the house and tell your father of his invitation and see what he says about it."[1] The boys went in and talked with Emir Harris, who was a brother of Martin Harris—one of the three witnesses of the Book of Mormon. Deeply troubled at the news, Emir told the boys he wanted to go to Joseph and lay the matter out before him. That night he trudged the two-and-a-half miles to Nauvoo.

"Brother Harris," the prophet began after listening intently to Emir's story. "I would advise you not to attend those meetings nor pay any attention to them. You may tell the boys, however, that I would like to have them go, but I want them to be sure to come and see me before the meeting takes place. I wish to give them some counsel."[2]

The boys readily agreed to obey, and on the following Sunday, met with Joseph. He asked them to attend the meeting that night and to pay strict attention to the proceedings. Then, at the first opportunity, they were to visit him without letting anyone know. The Prophet cautioned them to say as little as possible at the meeting and to avoid giving any offense.

Late that night, the boys walked to William Law's new brick house and found a large group of people. A number of men gave inflammatory speeches which were filled with innuendo and lies intended to prejudice the listeners against Joseph. The boys were frightened to realize that the group not only wanted to wrest all authority from Joseph Smith, but actually wanted to kill him.

Finally the meeting adjourned with plans to reconvene the

following Sunday. All present were firmly admonished not to tell a soul one word of anything that had been said. However, the boys were faithful, and at the first opportunity, bravely went to the Prophet and told him all that had occurred.

"Boys," Joseph said gravely. "I would like you to accept their invitation and attend the second meeting, but come to me again next Sunday, before their meeting convenes as I may have something more to say to you before you go."[3] They did and received more advice on how to handle themselves among the older men.

At the next meeting, the conspirators were even more vehement in their abusive remarks. New crimes had been discovered and old ones were magnified tenfold. Accusations were now also leveled against Hyrum and other prominent men in the Church. The meeting continued late into the night, with the leaders denouncing the prophet and accusing him of the most heinous crimes possible. All present, except Dennison and Robert, agreed to develop a more effective organization in order to take the Prophet's life.

Once again the young men managed to report back to Joseph without arousing the suspicions of anyone who had attended the meeting. "Boys, come to me again next Sunday," the Prophet said thoughtfully as they concluded their report. "I wish you to attend the next meeting also."[4]

They agreed to obey the Prophet, despite the growing danger to themselves. To protect themselves, the young men kept their connection with the murderous group a profound secret from all of their friends and most of their family. The next time Dennison and Robert met with the Prophet, he was seriously concerned about their welfare, knowing they were being placed in a very dangerous situation.

"This will be your last meeting," Joseph announced. "This will be the last time that they will admit you into their councils. They will come to some determination, but be sure," he cautioned, "that you make no covenants, nor enter into any obligations whatever with them. Be strictly reserved and make no promise either to conspire against me or any portion of the community. Be silent and do not take any part in their deliberations."[5]

Pausing a moment to think, Joseph added, "Boys, this will be their last meeting and they may shed your blood, but I hardly think they will, as you are so young. If they do, I will be a lion in their path! Don't flinch. If you have to die, die like men; you will be martyrs to the cause and your crowns can be no greater. But, I hardly think they will shed your blood."[6]

The interview was a long one. Joseph's sensitive feelings were touched by the faith and courage shown by these two valiant young men who were so willing to undertake such a hazardous enterprise on his behalf. The Prophet concluded their meeting by pronouncing a blessing upon Dennison and Robert. Laying his hands upon their heads, Joseph blessed them with safety, promised them rewards for their sacrifice and told them that if their lives were taken, their reward would be all the greater.

Dennison and Robert left Joseph's house, and with some trepidation, waited for evening. The prophet had made them see more clearly the great danger they were placing themselves in. If anyone present at the meeting knew they were reporting to Joseph or if they happened to do anything to arouse the slightest suspicion that they had been talking about the secret meetings, their lives would be snuffed out in a moment. Yet the boys determined to trust in the Lord and decided that they would rather die than betray the Prophet.

Finally, the time for the meeting came. Dennison and Robert were met and welcomed on the street by William Law and Austin Cowles. When they walked up the alley to enter the house, the young men were surprised to see men on each side of the narrow alley armed with muskets and bayonets. Men, similarly armed, were guarding the door. After being thoroughly searched and questioned, the young men were admitted. Inside, the house was in an uproar. Men were spouting forth a flood of accusations against Joseph. As the clamor of charges continued, expanding emotions that were already inflamed, it became clear that everyone was determined that Joseph should die. The only problem was that as yet, no one could agree upon how it should be done.

The rantings and ravings continued, with only Dennison and Robert remaining silent. Finally their quietness began to arouse suspicions. Every little while, Cowles would come and sit by Dennison, sliding an arm around his shoulder and asking how he felt. William Law did the same with Robert. The older man alternately argued and implored Robert to join their efforts. When pressed, Dennison did not lie and told Cowles frankly that he had been reared in the Church and that he had always esteemed Brother Joseph highly. Such defense of the Prophet aroused the anger of all present. Great pains were taken to point out—once again—the many great crimes

Joseph had committed. The men piously professed that they had only come to take such extreme measures for the good of the Church. To this, the boys replied that they were young, did not understand such matters and would rather not take part.

As the meeting proceeded, the boys were aghast to see that an oath had been prepared. A legal Justice of the Peace, Francis Higbee, sat at one end of the room, ready to administer the oath to every individual present. As each candidate stepped forward, they picked up a Bible.

As they raised the holy book in their right hand, Justice Higbee spoke in a chillingly official manner: "You solemnly swear before God and all holy angels and these your brethren, by whom you are surrounded, that you will give your life, your liberty, your influence, your all, for the destruction of Joseph Smith and his party, so help you God?"[7]

One by one the men intoned, "I do," and laying down the Bible, signed their name to a written copy of the oath. Dennison wondered how such men, having once enjoyed the light of truth, could fall into such depths of wickedness. Both boys worried about their own fate and dreaded the time when the last man would take the oath. Altogether, about two hundred men signed.

Cowles, Law and other men began arguing with Robert and Dennison once again to take the oath. They would not.

Dennison said, "We told them that we were young, that we were not members of the High Council, and that we knew nothing at all about their charges."[8] He continued, "We came to your meetings because we thought you were our friends and gave us a kind invitation. We did not think there was any harm in it, but if you will allow us to go now, we will not trouble any more of your meetings. Joseph Smith has never done us any harm and we do not feel like injuring him."

Another tirade was launched about the Prophet's wickedness, but the boys steadfastly refused to give in. "No," they said, "we cannot take an oath like that against any man who has never done us the least injury."[9]

The young men once again asked to leave, but a man in the back cursed them, shouting, "No, not by a _______ sight. You know all our plans and arrangements and we don't propose that you should leave in that style. You've got to take that oath or you'll never leave here alive."

"If you don't take that oath," one of the leaders avowed, "we will cut your throats."[10]

"Dead men tell no tales," another man cried.[11] As the mob surged toward them, Law and Cowles shouted for quiet, afraid that people on the street might hear and come to investigate. Then they tried once more to forcibly persuade the young men to change their minds and join with them. Finally, Dennison and Robert asserted that the dissenters would have to shed their blood before they would sign, and for a time, it appeared that such a fate would soon befall them.

Dennison said, "They then walked us off with one man on each side of us armed with sword and bowie knife and two men behind us with loaded guns, cocked, with bayonets on them."[12]

One chilling, last attempt to have Dennison and Robert

change their minds was made. "Boys, if you will take that oath your lives shall be spared; but you know too much for us to allow you to go free and if you are still determined to refuse, we will have to shed your blood."[13]

It was a terrible moment. Men armed with bowie knives and swords surrounded the boys and began to push them toward the cellar. Frightened and shaking, the boys eyed one another, but remembering Joseph's words, they would not back down. They had gone about fifteen feet when, like a miracle, they heard someone shout to stop.

"The boys' parents very likely know where they are," one man spoke up anxiously, "and if they do not return home, strong suspicions will be aroused and they may institute a search that would be very dangerous to us." The others knew this was true.

"It is already late and time that the boys were home," another voice agreed.[14]

The boys' hope rose as the men began to argue among themselves. Finally, it was decided that rather than murder them outright, it was safer to their cause to release the young men with strict orders not to reveal anything they had seen or heard. The boys were told that if they breathed a word of what had gone on in the meetings, they would be killed at first sight. This threat was repeated several times. Then, because some felt that many of the men were still intent on killing the boys, it was decided to send guards to escort them away from the house.

Once they were some distance away, the boys began to breathe easier—until the escorts forced them to go away from town, down a little-used road that led to the river. It soon became apparent that their "guards" were among those who felt that murdering the boys was the surest way to keep them silent.

However, at the last minute, one of the guards decided he was against murder. As the lone dissenter argued with the others, telling them to let the boys go with one last warning, Dennison and Robert were startled to see a ghostly hand rise out of the bushes a few yards distant and beckon to them. Concealing their surprise, they took off sharply in that direction when the sympathetic guard told them to run, thankful that no shots rang out as they raced along.

When they reached the bushes near the water, a body rose above the spot where the hand had been. It was Joseph Smith. Another body rose beside him—that of Joseph's bodyguard, John Scott, who was Robert's brother.

Joseph had become so worried that he had set out to find the boys. He and John had jumped in the bushes to hide when they heard the guards approach. Joseph ushered the boys a quarter of a mile further along the river. Just opposite his store, where a board fence met the river, he asked the young men to sit down in the shrubbery so that they might be well hidden as they talked.

"Boys, we saw your danger and were afraid you would not get out alive, but we are thankful that you got off safely. Now relate to me all that you have witnessed." As the boys gave a complete accounting, Joseph's face turned sorrowful. At the conclusion of their story, he groaned loudly in great distress and exclaimed, "O, brethren, you do not know what this will terminate in!" Then he burst into anguished tears.

Brother Scott, Joseph's trusted friend, came closer and threw his arms around the Prophet. He began to cry also and asked, "O, Brother Joseph, do you think they are going to kill you?"

A few minutes passed before Joseph managed to control his feelings. Then his face changed and looking thoughtful, said enigmatically, "I fully comprehend it." Then his countenance underwent yet another change and his voice became stern. "They accuse me of being a false prophet but I am no false prophet. . . . God has thus far dictated me and directed me and strengthened me in this work."[15]

To protect the young men, Joseph made them promise not to reveal what had happened to a living soul—not even to their own fathers—for at least twenty years. For Dennison's and Robert's personal safety, their heroic part in helping to keep the Prophet safe from harm had to remain a secret.

Dennison L. Harris later traveled across the plains to Utah. When he became a bishop in Monroe, Utah, he gave a verbal accounting of his experience to President Joseph F. Smith.

Notes

1. *The Contributor,* (Salt Lake City: Deseret News Company, 1884), p. 251.

2. Ibid., p. 252

3. Ibid.

4. Ibid., 253

5. Ibid.

6. "*Verbal Statement of Bishop Dennison L. Harris,*" (Salt Lake City: LDS Church Archives), p. 2.

7. Ibid, p. 3.

8. Ibid.

9. *The Contributor, op cit.*, p. 255.

10. Ibid., pp. 255–256.

11. "*Verbal Statement of Bishop Dennison L. Harris,*" *op cit.*, p. 3.

12. Ibid., p. 4.

13. *The Contributor*, 256.

14. Ibid, 256.

15. *Verbal Statement,* pp. 5–6.

Chapter 2

Martha & Wallace Toronto

FAITHFUL BEHIND THE IRON CURTAIN

Just one year after their marriage in 1934, Martha and Wallace Toronto were called to preside over the Czechoslovakia Mission. Wally was pleased, because as a young missionary, he had helped open up the new Czechoslovakia Mission.

The Torontos arrived in 1936 and, just two years later, began to feel the squeeze of Adolf Hitler's regime. When a takeover of Czechoslovakia's industrial region led to a round of false arrests and executions, Martha fled to Switzerland with their two children, twenty-month-old Bob and four-year-old Marion. They were able to return within a few months, but shortly afterwards, Germany invaded the country. After the takeover, the German armed forces showed off their military might and intimidated the local populace by flying their planes overhead, thundering their tanks down the streets, and goose stepping their troops down Wenceslaus Square.

Despite a growing dread of the Nazis, members of the Church continued to meet. On Mother's Day, the Church service was just drawing to a close when the back door opened. People turned around and gasped when they saw a tall Nazi officer in a striking white naval uniform boldly walk in. The entire congregation froze, as the imposing presence of a German officer usually meant one of two things: arrest or imprisonment. The officer hesitated briefly, then walked down the center aisle toward Elder Toronto who rose from the stand where he had been sitting and began talking with the visitor.

The frightened audience was motionless with apprehension when the officer approached the pulpit and began to speak. He introduced himself as Brother Schrul and said he was an elder in the Church. Brother Schrul said he knew they were startled to see an officer of the Third Reich, but hoped that during his military assignment in that city, they would allow him to worship with them. With great sighs of relief, the congregation welcomed him.

A few months later, in July of 1839, Sister Toronto took the trolley to attend a meeting of the Mutual Improvement Association, or MIA. When she arrived at the YMCA hall—where they held their meetings—the door was inexplicably locked. Normally, the missionaries arrived early to unlock the door and set up chairs. Another key was found but Wally and Martha worried about the absentee missionaries.

The next morning, a tall Gestapo agent in an immaculate black uniform knocked at the door of the mission home. The agent stepped in, followed by Asael Moulton, one of the four missing elders. The Gestapo agent told Elder Toronto that all four missionaries were being held prisoner. The agent had found a key in Asael's pocket and had come to see what it unlocked. During this explanation, Asael was not allowed to say a word.

Reluctantly, Wally brought out the metal box that the missionary's key would unlock. It contained American dollars that he had been saving in case his family had to flee unexpectedly. Brother Toronto was hesitant to open the box because it had recently become against the law to have American dollars for more than two weeks without converting them to local crowns. As the lid was being raised, Asael distracted his guard briefly, allowing Elder Toronto time to quickly slip one bundle of large bills into the desk drawer.

The German agent confiscated the box and the rest of the money, but refused to tell the mission president why the elders were being held. Later, Brother Toronto found out that the arrest had come about because of an incident that had happened weeks ago.

At that time, one of the missionaries—being pinpointed as an American—had been approached by an unidentified Gestapo agent who asked if the missionary wanted to exchange his dollars for German currency. Such an exchange seemed inconsequential at the time, but later a new monetary law was enacted that strictly forbade such transactions. Strangely enough, the law was made retroactive. This meant that even though the incident had occurred weeks before the law had gone into effect, the Nazis could still arrest the missionary who had made the exchange. In addition, the missionary's companion and two other elders who had the misfortune of stopping by the apartment while the Gestapo was still there were arrested as well.

The four young missionaries were confined in Pankrac, an infamous Gestapo prison. After their arrest, Sister Toronto went every week on the streetcar—a one-hour trip—to the prison gates to pick up the elders' laundry to take home to wash. Elder Toronto spent his days trying to get the missionaries released and had to depend heavily upon his wife to help run the mission. One of her duties was to make all the arrangements for a mission-wide conference. When Elder Joseph Fielding Smith arrived for that conference, he was concerned about the Church's precarious status in a Nazi-occupied country. He and Brother Toronto spent many hours planning and working out details in case the missionaries needed to be evacuated in the future.

Efforts to get the young men released did not go well. Wally wryly informed his wife that he was picking up a lot of new language from the colorful officers he encountered, even though he really didn't understand the words. Finally, the Germans said they would release the boys for $10,000—a veritable fortune. Brother Toronto refused such exorbitant demands and continued to negotiate for the young men's release.

One day, upon coming home after another long day at Gestapo headquarters, Brother Toronto told his wife, "I'm afraid I blew it today. I was so mad at Herr 'so-and-so' that I called him some terrible names and I don't know what they meant!" Pulling out his German dictionary, Brother Toronto took a few moments to look up the words. Sister Toronto busied herself in the room, then heard him exclaim, "Oh my!"[1] A few moments later, he was hard at work writing a letter of apology.

Through Elder Toronto's untiring efforts, the Gestapo finally agreed to release the four missionaries for $1,000. However, before they could be released, evacuation orders were received. All the missionaries left quickly and Sister Toronto and the children made plans to travel alone. Elder Toronto had to stay and make arrangements for the four imprisoned elders to leave as soon as they were freed.

President Smith had advised the mission president to keep approximately twenty-five dollars for each missionary in case of emergency. However, during the evacuation, each elder was only allowed to take ten crowns—the equivalent of one dollar and sixty cents—out of the country. The mission only had thirty missionaries. That left a considerable sum of money that desperately needed to be smuggled out so it could be used for the elders' traveling expenses when they returned to the United States. After prayerful consideration, Wally told his wife that the border guards would not likely suspect a woman with small children of smuggling and asked if she would carry the money.

Although she was frightened, Sister Toronto agreed and slipped $3,000 into her coat pocket. A friend had advised her that a pocket was less likely to be searched than a purse or suitcase. This same friend also gave money to the train conductor, asking him not to disturb Sister Toronto and the children when they got to the German border, which allowed Martha and her children to avoid being searched at the border.

Sister Toronto and her children arrived safely in Copenhagen where they were met by Elder Mark Garff, the Danish Mission President. Elder Joseph Fielding Smith and his wife, Jesse, were also there, helping direct the evacuation of seven hundred LDS missionaries from Europe.

Meanwhile, on the appointed day, Elder Toronto went to pick up the missionaries from the prison where they had spent a total of forty-four days. He exclaimed, "Oh, this was a happy day for all of us. So many anxious hours had been spent, so much negotiation and so much vain dealing to free them! But now they were free!"[2]

Unfortunately, their trial was not yet over.

When her husband did not arrive the next day with the missionaries as expected, Sister Toronto began to fear the worst. All news sources confirmed that war was to be announced at any minute and she knew that if war was declared before Wally could get out, he would not be allowed to leave at all. Anxiously, Sister Toronto watched the arrival of all the trains, ferries, and boats from Germany. Her nerves had reached the breaking point when official word came that no more transportation from Germany would be allowed into Denmark. Also, because war was so imminent, all communication with Czechoslovakia and other central European countries had been terminated. Distraught, Sister Toronto went to see President Joseph F. Smith.

He calmed her fears and gave her an inspired assurance.

"Sister Toronto," he declared, "this war will not start until your husband and those missionaries get on Danish soil."[3]

That night she received a phone call. It was her husband. Wally explained the reason for their delay. Shortly after the missionaries had been released, one of them had been re-arrested because he had the same last name as a British spy the Nazis were looking for. Brother Toronto told his worried wife that he had managed to straighten out the mix up just in time for him and the missionaries to leave Czechoslovakia with the British delegation on a train that had been sent especially for them. They had barely managed to board the last ferry out of Germany and were now on the coast, trying to arrange for transportation to Copenhagen.

They had escaped in the nick of time. Martha said, "Almost the minute Wally called Copenhagen from the coast, the war just exploded."[4] In fact, England and France declared war on Germany before Brother Toronto and the missionaries even arrived in Copenhagen. The Torontos returned to their home in Salt Lake City for the duration of the war.

Near the war's end, Brother Toronto received a letter from Joseph Roubicek, acting president of the Czech Mission. It was the first letter from the mission to reach the Church in five and a half years. Part of it read:

> "I wish to inform you that after six years of war all members of the Church have remained well and alive. It has been a terrible time. We have remained faithful, however, and we await you. . . . We often think of you and the missionaries. Here there is great need and distress. . . . Their testimo-

> nies of the truthfulness of the gospel have not wavered even in the worst moments of this great conflict. . . . If it is possible, please inform me when it will be possible to send missionaries and if you can come. The Czechoslovakian members stop every American that they see and ask him if he is from Utah or whether he is a Mormon."[5]

The war ended in 1945 and the following year, Elder Ezra Taft Benson, President of the European Mission, wrote in his journal: "Permission was granted for missionaries and a mission president from Zion to resume their proselytizing activities in this land. The Church enjoys a very favorable reputation."[6]

Elder and Sister Toronto were called into the office of the First Presidency and asked how they felt about going back to open up the Czech Mission and putting the pieces back together again so that the gospel could be preached. There were no doubts in their minds, especially since Wally had never been released. Brother Toronto flew to Czechoslovakia ahead of his family so that he could find a place for the mission home. Traveling with him were Elder Victor Bell, Elder Heber Jacobs, and a train car loaded with supplies from Church headquarters.

Much of Elder Toronto's time was spent trying to find Church members, many of whom had moved or been imprisoned. He found one sister, Frieda Glasnerova Vaneckova—a Jewish convert—in a hospital recovering from the two years she had spent in a concentration camp. She had lost eleven members of her family in the ovens at Auschwitz. Crying with joy at seeing him, Freida asked him to baptize her two boys. The emaciated woman told him that, after her release from the concentration camp, she had saved what she could for tithing. She gave it all to Elder Toronto.

It took a year for Brother Toronto to find a suitable place for his family to live. Travel arrangements were made, but before Sister Toronto left, she went to see President David O. McKay. After receiving a special blessing at the Prophet's hands, Martha and her five children went back to Czechoslovakia.

The new mission home was a large, three-story villa that had plenty of room for as many as sixteen missionaries who would stay there while they learned the language. Unfortunately, food was a big problem. The children were only allowed one-quarter liter of milk (about one glassful) per day. Each person was allowed two eggs, one pound of meat and one-fourth pound of sugar per month. Lines were long and plentiful, since there was one shop for meat, another for vegetables, etc. Sister Toronto took a pail whenever she went to stand in the milk line. After turning in her ration tickets, a man would then submerge a dipper the size of their allowance into an open tub of milk that had no protection from dirt or flies.

Despite physical hardships, the gospel surged forward. Sister missionaries began to arrive and soon new branches were opened. Despite another pregnancy, Sister Toronto presided over the Relief Society, dutifully sending monthly reports to Church headquarters.

Then, early in 1948, a coup took place and Czechoslovakia found itself shackled to a communist regime. Life changed dramatically. Wally and Martha Toronto were forced to register as aliens and report to the secret police every week.

New restrictions were placed on the Church. Before anyone was allowed to speak in a meeting, they had to submit a written copy of their speech to the police a minimum of six weeks before it was to be given. Usually, the talk was returned censored. Often, there were agents present in their meetings, carefully watching for anything that might be construed as treason. They were watched constantly. The instant the Torontos left the house, a person popped up to follow them. All of their activities were noted and reported to the police.

Some members were threatened for attending Church and a few were even asked to spy on Church leaders. A few distraught members came to the mission president in tears, explaining that the communists had told them that, if they did not comply, they could lose their jobs or have their already meager rations cut. Elder Toronto calmly advised them to go along with the secret service's requests.

The mission president's biggest problem was keeping missionaries, as false accusations of spying became more and more frequent. When such charges were leveled, the missionaries were forced to leave the country. Martha commented on this situation. "There was a lot of harassment. They (the communists) were so determined to get the Americans, especially the missionaries out of the country. They accused them of espionage, black marketing, distributing subversive literature, anything that could give them a reason to expel them."[7]

Elder Toronto had to spend most of his days in government offices asking for extensions for whichever missionaries had just received their notices of expulsion. After just one year, the missionary force was down to less than half. In addition, the time the missionaries had between receiving their notices and when they had to leave became shorter. Instead of giving the missionaries a time limit of two weeks to leave, it became three days, then twenty-four hours. Finally, after four difficult years, President McKay advised Brother Toronto to close the mission.

As the missionaries began leaving, Wally organized Czech leaders to carry on in his absence. Then, two missionaries disappeared. It was assumed they had been arrested but it took a few tense days to discover which prison they were in. Unexpectedly, an official called and told Sister Toronto that the young men could be released, but only if they would leave the country within two hours. Martha didn't have time to reach her husband, so she began making arrangements to fly the elders to Switzerland. By working frantically, she and was able to meet the deadline so they were not re-arrested.

Sister Toronto continued her own preparations to leave, although she worried about traveling alone through perilous territory with six children. She was also fearful about leaving her husband behind. One night during this anxious time, the secret police came to the house and asked to see Brother Toronto. Martha was heartsick, knowing the disappearance of many people began with such a visit. Finally, Wally came upstairs.

"Martha, I have to go with these men," he began. "I'm sure they want to question me about the two elders who were flown out to Switzerland." He paused, then handed her a packet. "I'll be back but in case I don't come back, I have everything here for you. Your tickets for trains and the ship are here, and the reservations are all made. Here is the money you'll need—crowns, dollars, and French francs. Take the children as planned tomorrow morning and get them home."[8]

Sister Toronto stood at the window, watching as her husband left the house, flanked on two sides by men who led him to a waiting car. To her great relief, he was only gone seven hours. When Elder Toronto escorted his family to the train station on March 1, 1950, a crowd of Church members was there to say goodbye. Each of them presented Sister Toronto with a little gift of food—items she knew they could neither afford nor spare from their meager rations. As the train pulled out, latecomers ran along side the train, handing little bundles of goodies through the open window, tears running down their cheeks.

At the Czech custom station, the officials not only went through the Torontos' suitcases, but opened every package they had been given. They broke open each sandwich, tore apart every roll, cut into each cake and crumbled all the cookies. They even cut up the apples, effectively ruining all the gifts that had been so lovingly prepared and given. Sister Toronto salvaged what she could for her children's dinner. The Toronto family was met in Paris by Dr. James L. Barker, the mission president of France and a short time later, they sailed for America.

Meanwhile, in Czechoslovakia, Brother Toronto laid future plans for the mission, knowing his expulsion was not far off. Then, the last two missionaries who had stayed behind to help, Elder Mabey and Elder Martini, were notified they had twenty-four hours to leave.

Elder Toronto had an important letter for the First Presidency that he had been unable to send and decided to give it to Elder Mabey to deliver. However, just before the missionaries left, Wally suddenly changed his mind. Taking the letter back, Brother Toronto gave it to Elder Martini instead, telling him to hide it under his sweater. Before the train even pulled out of the station, security guards took Elder Mabey off the train and stripped him to the skin for a thorough inspection before allowing him to reboard. Elder Martini was not searched.

Elder Toronto received his expulsion order, but was given a surprisingly long seven days notice. During this time, he appointed and set men apart to lead the three remaining branches of the mission. He then went to Switzerland, planning to run the mission from there. Unfortunately, his application to have the government recognize the Church was denied. The Latter-day Saints were forced to go underground. Feeling helpless, Brother Toronto returned to Salt Lake City.

During the following years, Brother Toronto filled out many applications for a visa so he could return to Czechoslovakia, but his name was too well known by the secret police as an "espionage agent" and each request was denied. Then, in 1964, President David O. McKay met with Elder and Sister Toronto.

"Our members (in Czechoslovakia) need you at this time," he proclaimed. "They have been carrying on underground long enough. They need the authority of their mission president. I advise that you and Sister Toronto go home, make application again, and if it's the Lord's will, He will open the way."

Obediently, the couple applied for the tenth time. In one week, their visas came back, allowing them to spend fifteen days in Czechoslovakia. Before they left, the Torontos met with President McKay who asked if there was anything they needed.

"Yes," President Toronto replied soberly, "we need a blessing. We need much courage and strength for this assignment."

"That you do," the Prophet responded and, with President Hugh B. Brown, gave a wondrous blessing of safety and help.[9] President Brown promised Sister Toronto that she would be blessed with a full recall of the language that she had forgotten.

The Torontos speeded up their Christmas plans, celebrating early with their children and twelve grandchildren before leaving on Christmas Day. Upon their arrival in Europe, they met with President Ezra Taft Benson. He advised them to report to an American embassy before they crossed the border, in case they didn't come back.

Sister Toronto began feeling somewhat anxious as they traveled toward Czechoslovakia, but after recalling the blessing of peace and help they had been given, felt more at peace. She and her husband were determined to do what President McKay had asked, to go quietly among the members, assure them that God was mindful of them and leave a blessing upon them.

As they approached the Czech station, Wally asked his wife to pray aloud to soften the hearts of the men at the gates of the border. The soldiers were armed with machine guns and would make the final decision about whether the Torontos entered the country or not. After much hesitation and a thorough examination, the guards allowed them to pass.

Sister Toronto felt a wave of fright as they crossed over and saw "No-Man's Land." This dreadful barrier surrounded the entire country of Czechoslovakia. It consisted of a cleared strip of barren ground 100 yards wide, which was patrolled with vicious dogs and lined with a high fence, topped with entanglements of sharp barbed wire.

Their last barrier was a stop at the guardhouse. They prayed that the guards would not open the "black book" and see Elder Toronto's name on it, as the secret police still thought he had been the leader of a spy ring. People inside the country had told the Torontos that Wally's picture was displayed in post offices, movie houses and other public places as a wanted criminal. Their prayers were answered. The book remained closed and the guards allowed them to pass.

There had been no way to inform local Church leaders about their visit. Such a letter would have been disastrous for the little group of underground saints. So that evening, the Torontos burst unannounced into the home of Elder Vrba, the branch president. A few nearby Saints excitedly spread the good news that their beloved mission president and his wife had returned and people gathered to rejoice. Tears flowed freely as old friends embraced.

During the happy reunion, Sister Vrba complimented Sister Toronto on her Czech, telling the American that she spoke as well as she did when she left. This surprised Martha. In all the excitement and confusion, she hadn't been aware that she was speaking the language perfectly.

The past years had been difficult for the Saints. Working underground made it hard for Elder Vrba to provide his charges with the sacrament. The ordinance had to be done regularly, yet stealthily, so that the brethren carrying the bread and water would remain undetected. Every week, Brother Vrba directed the brethren to go by twos into each home. They would teach the family a short lesson, administer the sacrament, then cautiously leave. It took all day for the priesthood to visit the homes. They changed districts and partners often to allay suspicions.

During their stay, the Torontos visited ten to fifteen houses a day, seeing as many of the members as they could. Brother Toronto blessed the sick, advanced men in the priesthood, made changes in branch presidencies, and along with his wife, strengthened the faith of the members.

"At each home we were greeted by tears of great joy," Martha stated. "Our people needed us and seeing us in person was a great moral booster for them. And we knew the Lord was protecting us, too, because we were not detained anywhere and were never approached by the police."

Before they left, Brother Vrba asked Sister Toronto to relay a message to President McKay. He said, "I want to thank him for sending you along with your husband."

"Why is that?" Martha asked in surprise.

"Because you have been an example to our women. Our wives are afraid and won't let us go when we have assignments. We know there are dangers, but now they have seen you, and your assignment with your husband has been far more precarious than ours, yet you have gone with him under very trying circumstances and they have seen how you share in the priesthood."[10]

Back in the United States, Brother and Sister Toronto continued to do what they could to aid the Czech Saints. Then, in 1965, Elder Toronto was able to visit the country one more time, although this time, Sister Toronto remained in the United States. He would travel alone and planned to meet with government officials and plead with them to recognize the Church.

Midway during his visit, Elder Toronto was falsely accused and arrested. In an ironic twist, his arrival at police headquarters enabled him to meet with the very officials he had previously tried—and failed—to meet. Because of his arrest, which turned out to be a blessing in disguise, Wally was able to ask the officials if they would allow The Church of Jesus Christ of Latter-day Saints to meet together openly. Although his request was denied, Brother Toronto was able to successfully defend himself against the false charges and he was freed.

Elder and Sister Toronto's efforts, along with the work and prayers of many faithful and dedicated people, finally bore fruit. In January of 1990, the government officially recognized The Church of Jesus Christ of Latter-day Saints. In July of that same year, the Church formally reestablished the Czechoslovakia Prague Mission.

Notes

1. Martha Toronto Anderson, *A Cherry Tree Behind The Iron Curtain, The Autobiography of Martha Toronto Anderson*, (Salt Lake City: LDS Church Archives), pp. 24–25.

2. Wallace Felt Toronto, "*Journal 1936 May 1939 Oct.*" (Salt Lake City: LDS Church Archives), p. 79.

3. Martha Sharp Anderson, "*Interview, Salt Lake City, Utah 1978,*" (Salt Lake City: LDS Church Archives), p. 2.

4. Ibid., p. 3

5. "First Report Comes From Czechoslovakia," *Church News*, 21 July 1945, p. 9.

6. Ezra Taft Benson, *A Labor of Love, The 1946 European Mission of Ezra Taft Benson,* (Salt Lake City: Deseret Book, 1989), p. 70.

7. Martha Sharp Anderson, "Interview, Salt Lake City, Utah 1978," op cit., p. 4.

8. Martha Toronto Anderson, *A Cherry Tree Behind The Iron Curtain, The Autobiography of Martha Toronto Anderson, op cit.*, p. 61.

9. Ibid., pp. 77–78

10. Ibid., pp. 93–95

Chapter 3

Sale Manu

"Be The Father That I Was!"

Sale Manu, along with his wife and eleven children, were called as missionaries and asked to go to Western Samoa. Their assignment was to start a branch in the little village of Sataupaii. Although the Mormons were disliked and faced much persecution, Brother Manu worked hard to teach the gospel in Sataupaii.

One minister, however, was particularly hostile to the Mormon missionaries. When he found out that some of his own congregation had converted to this new religion, he became so furious that he gathered together a mob to go after Sale. When they went to the Manu home and found it empty, they began searching the village. Finally, the mob found the family walking down the road. The Manus had been visiting someone who was ill and were on their way home. The incensed minister, his eyes on his quarry, made his way to Sale by pushing aside the children, some of whom fell to the ground.

Crowding Sale up against a tree, the preacher held a machete to his throat and roared, "Why do you steal my sheep?"

"Because you deceive this people and you do not know what is the truth," Brother Manu answered promptly. Angrily the minister warned Sale that he and all his family would be killed if they did not deny this Mormon religion. Sale would not cower.

"I will not deny that Joseph Smith is a prophet of God," he declared firmly. The minister's threats were not carried out, but the persecution continued. Finally the village high chief grew weary of the strife and issued an edict to Sale: "Leave the village or die."[1]

The chief gave the family a deadline for compliance. They had until December 25th to leave the area. Worried, Sale decided to seek advice from his priesthood leader. He paddled his outrigger canoe two days and two nights to see President John Adams. Elder Adams told Sale to pray about the matter and assured him that the Lord would answer his petition. Another two days and nights were spent on the water in prayerful petition as Sale made his way back to the island. When he arrived home, Brother Manu knew what he was going to do. He gathered his anxious family around him.

"It is the Lord's will that we stay on this island and in this village, and if necessary, seal our testimonies with our own blood that we do know Joseph Smith was a prophet of God."[2]

The family accepted his decision.

So it was, that on the day before Christmas in 1945, a mob descended on the Manu home. They pulled up pineapple trees, chopped down others and completely destroyed the garden. With the deadline nearly at hand, Sale and his family were warned one final time that they had until the morning to be gone. If they did not leave, the chief had ordered them to be burned alive.

On Christmas morning, the Manu family dressed in their best clothes and knelt together, praying for deliverance. The mob arrived and torched their home. Quickly, Sale evacuated his family, taking them behind the blazing house to the cookhouse, but the mob set that structure on fire too. Then, as the family watched, the mob lit a tremendous bonfire between the two burning buildings. The high chief spoke directly to Sale, admonishing him to leave the village or suffer the consequences. Faithful to the gospel, Sale refused to back down.

"I am here because my Church is true and I will never deny my testimony," he told the crowd who had to strain to hear above the crackle of the bonfire. "I am ready to die and seal my testimony that I do know that the Mormon Church is the true Church of God."

"Sale Manu," the chief grimly warned, "I gave you a chance to save your life and the lives of your family. What do you have to say?"

"We are ready to die!" Sale spoke defiantly. No one moved or spoke. Sensing a change in the old man's feelings, Brother Manu asked, "What are you waiting for?" The high chief hesitated and his face changed, as if some great battle was raging within himself. His expression softened. When he spoke, his voice was tremulous.

"Now I know that you are a man of God," the chief choked, "and I cannot do this great thing."[3] With that solemn pronouncement, the villagers began leaving. Eventually, the bonfire burned itself out.

That night the high chief, along with the bitter minister and forty other people was arrested. When the time came for the trial, the room was packed with spectators waiting to hear what Brother Manu would say about his persecutors. After all the evidence had been presented, Sale was brought forward.

Speaking solemnly, the judge said, "Whatever you declare to be a just punishment for these men, including years of imprisonment, I will grant you. There will be religious freedom in these islands."

Sale said quietly, "I forgive them. Let them go home to their families with the understanding that they leave the Latter-day Saints alone." Many were surprised at his forgiveness toward the men who had wanted to kill not only him, but his wife and children as well. The judge quietly accepted his decision. "From this time forth the Latter-day Saints may preach anywhere on the island," he decreed, "and if they have enough people to build a chapel, they may surely do it."[4]

Inspired by the courage of Sale and his family, hundreds of villagers investigated the gospel and joined the Church during the next few months. In time, all but a few in the village were baptized. With such tremendous growth, there was a great and immediate need for a new chapel. Brother

Manu was asked to choose a site for the new structure. After some thought, he took them to the spot in front of his house where the chief had ordered the bonfire built. He looked grimly at the blistering coals that had forever marked the ground and made his decision. A new ward chapel was built upon the ashes of the fire made to consume Sale Manu and his family. Still standing today, it was for many years one of the largest buildings in Western Samoa.

Sale Manu spent the rest of his life going from village to village, teaching people the gospel. His last assignment was serving as a branch president in Fagomalo, the same village where he had been born. While there, he made the acquaintance of a subchief who was very interested in the Church, but could never quite bring himself to take the final step of baptism. They became good friends and one day the man made a promise.

"Sale Manu," he said. "If you will be faithful to the end of your days, I will join the Church."[5]

To make sure this promise was kept, Sale bought a burial plot that faced his friend's front door. After Sale died, his grave served as a reminder of this promise and proved to be the nudge the subchief needed to come into the Church. He and all of his family were baptized and later, the subchief took Sale's place as branch president.

Samoa has the distinction of being the first country in the world to be entirely organized into stakes of Zion. Although everyone there tries to raise their families to be strong and stalwart in the faith, none can surpass the example that Sale set for his children. Just before this great man died, he spoke a sermon to his son in a few simple words.

"Sekeli," he said firmly, "you be the kind of father that I was!"[6] ©*The Church of Jesus Christ of Latter-day Saints. Used by Permission.*

Notes

1. John Lewis Lund, "Leave the Village or Die!" *The Ensign*, February 1976, p. 32.

2. Ibid., 33.

3. Ibid.

4. Ibid.

5. Ibid.

6. Ibid.

Chapter 4

A. C. Christensen

"FEED MY SHEEP"

At the beginning of World War II, the war went badly for the United States in the Pacific. Finally, the Air Corps on the small island of Luzon in the Philippines was ordered to surrender. As A. C. Christensen, a twenty-year-old private, was taken away to a prisoner-of-war camp, he was unaware that he would be facing years of starvation and deprivation.

It was an abrupt change of circumstances for a young man who had left San Francisco just six months before. A. C. had arrived in the Philippines on Thanksgiving Day of 1941, little knowing that his quick meal of hot dogs and sauerkraut would be a feast he would dream about in the coming months. Shortly after the bombing of Pearl Harbor, the island of Luzon was hit by heavy enemy fire. The withdrawal of General

Douglas MacArthur from the Philippines in March of 1942 led to the capitulation of A. C.'s squadron two months later.

Piling into trucks marked with the white flags of surrender, A. C. and the rest of his unit were driven to a prisoner-of-war camp where they were thoroughly searched. Most of them, however, weren't wearing much more than shorts because of the heat and humidity. As they piled off the trucks, a guard pointed his bayonet at A. C.'s wrist, quickly persuading the young man to give up his watch. However, Brother Christensen did manage to hide away two pieces of paper—items that later meant the difference between life and death.

His life as a POW began—marked by lice, disease, occasional beatings and most of all, ever—present hunger. Rations for the prisoners consisted of approximately three-fourths of a cup of cooked rice, along with half a cup of soup, which was often made from weeds or fish heads. A few men thought of escaping, but not many dared attempt it after two Filipino prisoners who tried it were captured and brought back to camp. The POWs were assembled to watch as the two escapees were tied up and shot to death.

The prisoners' duties were many and varied. They dug ditches, gathered wood, repaired the roads and worked in the rice fields. Throughout it all, they were hungry.

"I would have gladly taken the chance of a beating for an extra mouthful of food," A. C. remarked, adding that the men were always on the lookout for something to fill their empty stomachs. "If a dog, cat or snake got in the compound," A. C. said cryptically, "it never left."[1] When their work took them into the jungle, they would pick the little red peppers that grew wild. If a prisoner was fortunate enough to have a small bottle, he would put the peppers inside, add some salt and water and have a sauce to flavor his rice.

Brother Christensen spent two and a half years in captivity in the Philippines. By then, the American front had advanced so far that the Japanese were forced to move the prisoners. During the move, the POWs' shoes were taken and they were blindfolded and securely tied. They were then put aboard a cargo ship—the kind used to transport cattle—and forced down into the hold.

On the way to Japan, they not only suffered from meager rations but also from lack of water. Brother Christensen and his comrades were only allowed one canteen cup of water a day—about one pint—which was soon used up in perspiration. The POWs also worried about being torpedoed by unsuspecting American ships because their ship was not marked—as it should have been—as one carrying prisoners of war. Such a danger was very real, as Allied forces had, on more than one occasion, innocently attacked unmarked ships carrying prisoners of war.

During the journey, the ship's engines kept breaking down. Despite the wait, A. C. found that stopping at nearby islands for repairs was actually a blessing. Each time, after repairs had been completed, the captain would hoist the anchor and blow steam out the pipes. As the steam cooled, water would condense inside the pipes. By opening the petcock, the prisoners could collect the moisture, allowing them a few extra swallows of water that day.

It took ninety days to reach Japan. Each day was spent in the dreary, dark hold of the ship that held approximately five hundred men. When they finally arrived at the camp, A. C. hungrily watched a Japanese guard peel an apple. The guard was well aware of the covetous looks the starving prisoners gave his apple. Watching them impassively, he let the luscious strips fall onto the ground where he stepped on them and ground them into the dirt.

"I would have given a lot for just one of those peelings," A. C. lamented.[2]

The POWs worked every day except Sunday. On that day, Brother Christensen met with others for worship service. Weekdays were spent laboring in a factory that was situated on the beach. During the winter, it was bitterly cold. At first, the men tried to keep a fire going by pilfering wood and sneaking it inside, but soon, even that small comfort was forbidden.

The men suffered from the cold at night since the only blankets they had were thin and stiff. Lice and bed bugs were common problems and caused constant irritation. Although there were public bathtubs, there was no soap and since the water wasn't changed until everyone had finished bathing, it wasn't good to be last in line.

Being allowed to write home was a blessing. However, the prisoners were given strict guidelines. The letter had to be less than twenty-five words, typewritten or block printed, and completely nonmilitary. A. C. was glad that his family, after wondering about his fate for years, would find out he was alive, but as it turned out, they never received any of his letters.

Hunger continued to cause the POWs their greatest suffering. If their guard chanced to wander away, the men would rush to the nearby beach and gather orange rinds, lettuce leaves or anything else that was even halfway edible that had washed up on the shore. When the men walked back to their barracks after a day's work, they would pluck weeds alongside the trail to lay atop their tiny serving of rice. Often, they would drink large quantities of water to fool their stomachs into thinking they were fuller than they actually were.

Malnutrition began causing a variety of diseases. The men were plagued with dysentery, malaria, beri-beri, dengue fever and scurvy. If a prisoner got sick and couldn't work, his rations were cut in half that did little to speed the invalid's recovery. There were several doctors among the POWs but they had no medicine.

Although he was being held captive in a foreign land, Brother Christensen never had any ill feelings toward his Japanese guards. He said, "I felt we were all victims of circumstance—we were all caught in a bad situation. I always felt the Japanese had good and bad among them just like the Americans."

Some of the guards showed real compassion as evidenced by the following experience. A. C. relates: "One of the things that stands out in my mind the most is an old man who tended the boiler at the copper factory. We all drank hot, boiled water and one day as I went to get my canteen filled, this old man shared his baked potato with me. I was really touched and realized that we are all human beings."[3]

By 1944, Brother Christensen had been in five different

prisons and survived years of anguish and hardship. But finally, he came to the point where his mind and body felt beaten beyond his ability to endure. One day he was weakly struggling to break up slag when he decided he could not work one moment longer. Laying down his hammer, A. C. told his astonished guard he would work no more. The guard took him aside and beat him severely.

Afterwards, A. C. could barely walk but somehow, made it back to his barracks. Sick and tired of fighting for survival, Brother Christensen lay on his bed, feeling unable to go on. He knew what would happen. He had seen others who had given up. Although such men weren't always the most ill, when they lay in their beds and curled up into a near-fetal position, they were almost always dead by morning.

As he lay on his hard cot, weak, bruised, and hungry, A. C. pulled out the two priceless pieces of paper he had managed to keep hidden for three years. One was a picture of his parents. The other was his patriarchal blessing, given to him by his grandfather and handwritten by his mother, who had taken down the words one by one.

As he read the words that she had so carefully written, Brother Christensen felt a small surge of hope take hold within. He began to wonder what the future might hold. Pulling out the picture, he carefully searched his parents' faces. Memories of his childhood began permeating through his current pain and anguish. A. C. remembered his loving home, his three brothers and four sisters and the happy times he had spent riding horses.

Strengthened in an undefinable way, Brother Christensen

began to pray. As he did, he remembered that Helaman's army of stripling warriors possessed unusual strength and courage because they had been taught so well and so righteously by their mothers. Although his own dear mother had died years ago, a promise that she had given A. C. and his brother came to him. He recalled that she had told her two sons that if they would live the Word of Wisdom, the Lord would bless them. Weakened by hunger and weighing only 85 pounds, A. C. didn't feel at that moment that he could run and not be weary, but perhaps, he thought, he could walk and not faint. His spirits were lifted as Heavenly Father blessed him with spiritual fortitude. A. C. made the decision to endure.

In the following days and weeks, whenever he felt down, Brother Christensen would get out his precious papers and read them over and over until he felt strengthened enough to be able to hang on just a little while longer. Unknown to him, his family—who had not heard from him in three years—were praying daily for his well being. His grandfather, who had given him his patriarchal blessing, had felt the reassuring promptings of the Spirit and had promised the worried family that A. C. was alive and would return one day.

Then, A. C. began seeing U.S. bombers streak by in the sky. Air raids became frequent. At night, American planes dropped bombs nearby and, in the distance, A. C. and his comrades could hear the horrific cries and moans of the injured.

Suddenly, the role of the guards changed. Instead of making sure the American prisoners did not leave the compound, they made sure that the no one broke *into* the camp.

The local people were enraged at the destruction rained upon them by Allied aircraft and consumed with grief when loved ones were killed during the bombing raids. If the guards had not protected the POWs', the angry populace would have stormed the compound, seeking revenge on the hapless prisoners.

At last, the long awaited day arrived. One of the guards told the men that the Japanese had surrendered. When the emaciated POWs knew their trials were almost over, they yelled, shouted, cried, and hugged each other in overwhelming exultation.

"I felt like Heavenly Father had truly protected me," Brother Christensen commented.[4] The men marked the roofs of their barracks with the letters P-O-W, so that the Americans could recognize them from the air. Supplies began floating down from the sky in brightly colored parachutes of orange, blue, red, and purple.

"It was a great day," A. C. recalled with a grin. "It was better than Christmas, Thanksgiving, and the Fourth of July all rolled into one."[5]

A. C. continued to keep the Word of Wisdom. He was especially glad of his decision when one POW decided to celebrate their release by drinking sake, a Japanese liquor. The sake had been poisoned and the man died before being able to return to the United States.

After arriving back in America, Brother Christensen spent some time in a rehabilitation center in California, then returned home to Tremonton, Utah. He renewed his acquaintance with a pretty young woman named Doris whom he had known in high school. They began dating and after a time, were married in 1947. As the years passed, A. C. continued to stay active in the Church. He served in the Sunday School, MIA, High Council, and later as a bishop.

After their son, Timothy, filled a mission to Hong Kong, A. C. and Doris felt a desire to serve a mission themselves. They filled out the paper work and waited anxiously, wondering where they would be called. A. C. went to the mailbox one day to find that he would be returning to the land where he had been held prisoner forty-five years ago—Japan. Although some POWs remained bitter against their captors, Brother Christensen declared that he never harbored any ill feelings toward the Japanese people. Indeed, he was eager to return.

Grinning, A. C. admitted, "I always wanted to go back." Then he smiled and added, "You know, people don't start wars, governments do. You always have to love people."[6]

Elder and Sister Christensen were the second adult couple to be called to Japan. Ironically, the husband of the first couple to serve a mission there had also been a prisoner of war in Japan.

During his first, involuntary trip to Japan, A. C. had suffered many hardships. This time, he had a far different experience.

"As exquisite as had been my hunger pains then, there was nothing now so exquisite as my joy in sharing the gospel with God's children in Japan," Brother Christensen declared. "Hadn't the Savior once said, 'Feed my sheep?' No longer would thoughts of Japan bring famine to mind. This time I anticipated a spiritual feast."[7] Doris and A. C. enjoyed a physical feast as well. Kind neighbors and friends were forever showering them with gifts of rice, fruit, and vegetables.

"During all the time we were there," Sister Christensen commented, "we only had to buy one ten-pound sack of rice. We were treated as honored guests."[8]

The Christensens lived in a farming area that had one small branch. Their living quarters were adjacent to an elementary school. The couple found it most appropriate and amusing when the little children on the playground began singing one of their favorite songs to the tune of "When the Saints Come Marching In."

One of their assignments was to locate inactive members and reactivate them. If they contacted someone who was interested in learning about the gospel, they would ask the younger missionaries to accompany them on subsequent visits.

Elder and Sister Christensen had a great desire to have people read the Book of Mormon but were unsure how to go about this, as most of the people they talked to were very reluctant to accept the book. However, A. C. and Doris soon discovered that many Japanese people had a great thirst for knowledge. They used that desire to their advantage, telling people that the Book of Mormon contained a history of an ancient people who lived in the Americas. As a result, the Christensens quadrupled the number of books they were able to give away.

Then the innovative couple had another idea on how to give more copies of the Book of Mormon away. Since almost everyone in Japan was trying to learn English, they decided to offer free English lessons. Naturally, they used the Book of

Mormon as their primer. The younger missionaries attended this club, or "circle" as it was called in Japan, and helped the members learn English. If a conscientious student wanted to study at home, the missionaries were quick to offer them a free copy of the Book of Mormon to take with them.

Once, a girl asked Elder and Sister Christensen if they would accompany her to a ladies club and speak to the group. The couple took advantage of that opportunity and was able to pass out more than a dozen copies of the Book of Mormon.

Occasionally during their stay, the subject of A. C.'s past imprisonment would come up. When acquaintances found out that Brother Christensen had been a prisoner of war in Japan and learned of his great trials, they would sometimes weep in sympathy. Twice during their mission, A. C. was asked to speak at firesides to a people whose government had once held him prisoner. He was thankful for those opportunities and taught the people that God loves all nationalities.

"I feel those fireside opportunities reached more people than our individual missionary efforts and was living proof of the gospel in action," Doris commented.[9]

The Christensens enjoyed a successful mission and returned home feeling that they had been spiritually fed.

After returning from his mission, Brother Christensen continued to share his war time experiences with many people. He has given over a hundred talks at firesides or in sacrament meetings. Standing as a quiet example of courage and endurance, A. C. continues to bear testimony of the truth and is quick to bear witness that Heavenly Father watches over all of us and has a great love for all of His children.

Notes

1. Personal Interview with A. C. and Doris Christensen, October, 1996.
2. Ibid.
3. Ibid.
4. Ibid.
5. Ibid.
6. Ibid.
7. Ibid.
8. Ibid.
9. Ibid.

Chapter 5

Cong Ton Nu Tuong-Vy

TRANSLATING BY THE SPIRIT

Living the life of a hermit in an old cave that had once been a tiger's den was the only existence that promised safety for Cong Ton Nu Tuong-Vy. Hunted by the North Vietnamese, Tuong-Vy hid while trying to find a way to leave Vietnam and reach the United States.

Tuong-Vy was born in Hue, the ancient capital of Vietnam, in 1923. Born of royal ancestry, her last name, Cong Ton Nu, is a title meaning "countess." As a child, Tuong-Vy lived in a spacious palace. She graduated from school when she was twenty, married a few months later and eventually had four daughters and two sons. She moved to Saigon in 1950 and fifteen years later she and her husband divorced. Tuong-Vy taught high school for the next five years, then began working for a travel service business.

In 1967, Robert J. Lewis, a member of The Church of Jesus Christ of Latter-day Saints, went to Tuong-Vy's office and asked if she knew of someone who could translate the pamphlet, *The Testimony of Joseph Smith*. She found a man who was willing to translate it, but when Elder Lewis took the booklet to Church, the Vietnamese members had difficulty understanding it.

Brother Lewis returned the pamphlet, hoping the translator could try again. When the man said he couldn't do any better, Tuong-Vy decided to try translating it herself, even though she was not good at speaking English. She took the pamphlet home one evening and found it so fascinating that she stayed up all night reading about Joseph Smith.

She said, "As I read, something strange happened to me. It was as if someone unseen was helping me understand. . . . I translated according to the thoughts and feelings impressed upon me. I did not know it at the time, but I was translating by the Spirit." When Brother Lewis gave his members this new translation, they understood it.

"It communicates feelings," they said approvingly. "It affects us."[1]

Excited with this success, Brother Lewis asked Tuong-Vy if she would translate other pamphlets. As she worked, Tuong-Vy became acquainted with the doctrines of the Church and came to love its teachings. Finally, she asked Brother Lewis to send the missionaries to teach her the gospel. After three months, she was baptized. Soon after, Tuong-Vy was called to be Relief Society president. Her oldest son, Le Phuc-Hung joined the Church a few months later. During that time, she became the owner of the travel service where she had been employed.

Then, in 1970, Sister Cong Ton Nu was given a new calling—to translate the Book of Mormon. Humbled and thrilled, she wondered how she could accomplish such a great task and still earn a living. Her office was too noisy and she had no time to spare in between directing ten secretaries, drivers and helpers. Tuong-Vy couldn't translate at home either, as her six children and their families lived with her and the noise would not allow her to think and study. She prayed for help in solving the dilemma.

An answer came through her son, Le Viet Hung, who had recently joined the military. One morning, he came home and dropped 400,000 piasters into his astonished mother's lap. He had won the money in a government contest. Here was the answer to her prayers. Tuong-Vy gathered her family around to make a momentous announcement.

"I give to you my home and all that I own. I take only this amount from the contest. I will quit my job and buy some land in a remote area."[2]

Forsaking everything in order to accomplish her calling to translate the Book of Mormon, Sister Cong Ton Nu left her spacious five-story home, children, and grandchildren and built herself a small cottage in a quiet area. She went into seclusion, studying day and night. She read the English version of the Book of Mormon a number of times. Because her French was better than her English, Tuong-Vy also studied the French version. Whenever she ran into difficulty, she would ask a relative, who was a priest in the Catholic Church, to help her understand the meaning of certain passages.

Tuong-Vy spent countless hours pondering and praying as she struggled to translate difficult sections. Often she would dream at night about the complex passages and wake inspired to know which books in her library would help her continue her important work.

"I don't know how I was able to translate the book," Tuong-Vy professed, "but Heavenly Father helped me. It was almost as if someone else was helping me write it."[3]

Translating the Book of Mormon took two long years. Then the dedicated woman turned her attention to translating the Doctrine and Covenants. Next came the Pearl of Great Price.

In 1975, there was a great political upheaval when South Vietnam fell to North Vietnam. Although Tuong-Vy had started translating other documents, she was unable to finish them. When the missionaries had to leave the country, Sister Cong Ton Nu gave them the documents she had finished and they were taken to Salt Lake City to Church headquarters. Soon, Tuong-Vy's text of the Book of Mormon was in print.

Then Tuong-Vy received a call from the American Embassy giving her directions on where and how she could leave the country. Although she was grateful for the opportunity, Sister Cong Ton Nu loved her country and felt confused at the thought of leaving.

"My Heavenly Father had given me great blessings in that land," Tuong-Vy explained, "so I felt loyal to it and decided to stay behind."[4]

However, when the North Vietnamese completed their takeover of Saigon, they not only imprisoned all South Vietnam government officials, but also jailed the president of her branch, all her brothers, one son, and a son-in-law. Because of her many contacts with Americans, the authorities decided to arrest Tuong-Vy. Realizing that she was no longer safe in her own country, Sister Cong Ton Nu decided to escape. But first, she went to an island and buried all her scriptures, translations, and books on a beach. Then she bought a boat and left. Unfortunately, Tuong-Vy's attempt to flee failed. She was captured and imprisoned for three days.

She was able to get out of jail, but for the next five years, Tuong-Vy had to use all her strength and resources to hide from authorities as she continued to try to leave the country. Changing her name and using various disguises, Sister Cong Ton Nu found places to live near the sea, hoping to leave the country by boat. On one of her attempts, Tuong-Vy was one of eighty men, women, and children who were trying to leave Vietnam. After traveling two days, they were jubilant to reach international waters. Then, the engine gave out.

"We drifted for fifteen days," relates Sister Cong Ton Nu. "We ran out of food and drinking water and just lay motionless on the deck awaiting death. Finally, we heard the noise of a ship's engine. We waved for help. It was a ship from Europe. After giving us food and water, they towed our boat back to Vung-Tau harbor. We wept openly. Many men, unable to accept the disaster, jumped into the sea and disappeared underwater. The police imprisoned us. Luckily I spent only a few months in jail."[5]

On her last attempt, Tuong-Vy was with a group of twenty people. Just as they started to board the boat, guards spotted them. Frightened, the people scattered in all directions as the soldiers gave chase. Tuong-Vy and two other women climbed a hill and hid in a cave. Later, the two women left, but Sister Cong Ton Nu was tired of running.

"I was so weary from the fears of the past years and so despairing that I didn't want to move anymore. I chose to stay."[6]

The shelter had a cement floor, some broken furniture and a few cooking utensils. The doors that someone had installed at the entrance to the cave were still in good condition. The best discovery, though, was a large deserted garden nearby. It was filled with fruit trees containing mangoes, longans, apples, and jackfruit. Still, her hideout was a lonely, deserted place and Tuong-Vy was frightened during her first night alone. To still her fears, she knelt down on a rock to pray.

"Through my tears and my loneliness, I asked Father in Heaven to give me the courage and strength to survive this ordeal. A peace and calm came upon me, and I knew that I could remain there. This is my testimony of prayer. Whenever I have been upset or have struggled, I have prayed. Heavenly Father always hears and answers my prayers. He always listens to his children."[7]

So began Sister Cong Ton Nu's solitary life. She took on a new disguise, shaving her head and disguising herself as an old, poor Buddhist nun. To obtain the few necessities her isolated life required, she would go to the market and exchange the ripened fruit she gathered in her orchard. In the village, she learned that her home was called the tiger's den because of the animal that used to live there before the villagers drove it out.

Every sunset found Tuong-Vy sitting on a rock, looking out over the Pacific. "I often imagined that on the other side of the water was our Heavenly Father's temple, near which many of my brothers and sisters were living in happiness. I couldn't help but weep, remembering the wonderful times I had had with my fellow Saints in the Saigon chapel."[8]

Years passed and Tuong-Vy became used to the silence, spending her time tending a small garden and writing songs, poems, and books. None of her children knew where she was and no one in the area knew who she really was. Two of her children were still in Vietnam and, although Tuong-Vy wrote them letters, she couldn't receive any as she had no address. She did not dare confide in anyone, feeling that such information would only bring trouble upon them.

Four long years had passed when Sister Cong Ton Nu became ill. Her condition became so bad that she had to go to the hospital. In the office, Tuong-Vy submitted her health card, the only document she had with her real name on it. A woman who was standing nearby read it.

Stepping closer, the stranger asked, "Are you Mrs. Cong Ton Nu Tuong-Vy?" Alarmed, Tuong-Vy started to back away, but the woman smiled and gestured for her to follow. In the lobby, the woman took a wrinkled letter from her handbag and gave it to Tuong-Vy.

It read; "My dear Sister Thuy, you should try to find Mrs. Cong Ton Nu Tuong-Vy, who we think is living somewhere near the Vung-Tau seashore. The Church of Jesus Christ at Salt Lake City wants to contact her. Signed, Quoc-Phong."[9] Tuong-Vy burst into tears. With the help of Sister Thuy, she was able to re-establish contact with the Church in Saigon.

That Christmas was a new beginning, as Tuong-Vy met with Church members in Saigon for the first time in ten years. Humbly, she received the sacrament from the priesthood brethren and began associating with members from that small branch. Finally, Sister Cong Ton Nu was able to send a message to Church headquarters. Then, with her oldest son sponsoring her, she was finally given permission to leave Vietnam. In less than one year after coming out of her cave, Tuong-Vy was able to come to the United States. She visited Salt Lake City and attended General Conference.

"The first time I saw Temple Square," she relates, "I could not help but weep for my blessings. In the Tiger's Den, it had been my greatest wish to see the temple. At last, I was able to receive my endowment in the Lord's house. Although I am now in America," Tuong-Vy concludes, "the memory of my experiences in Viet Nam stays with me. I know by personal experience that nothing can destroy the gospel our Heavenly Father has given us."[10] *©The Church of Jesus Christ of Latter-day Saints. Used by Permission.*

Notes

1. Cong Ton Nu Tuong-Vy, "Out of the Tiger's Den," *The Ensign*, June 1989, p. 45.

2. Ibid., p. 46

3. Ibid.

4. Ibid.

5. Ibid., pp. 46–47

6. Ibid., 47.

7. Ibid.

8. Ibid.

9. Ibid.

10. Ibid.

Chapter 6

Ellis Shipp

PIONEER DOCTOR

Did William Reynolds know great things were in store for his infant daughter when, after she stopped breathing, he rushed outside and began swinging her back and forth to revive her?

"Ellis," he cried after she'd been given an overdose of paregoric, "we will not let you die. You must stay with us, Ellis, you must live! You must live!"[1]

Ellis Reynolds Shipp did recover. Born in January, 1847, Ellis was still a child when missionaries taught her family about the restored gospel. She and her family were baptized members of The Church of Jesus Christ of Latter-day Saints and traveled west across the plains. They settled in Utah Valley where Ellis learned the value of hard work, a principle that would prove beneficial in later years.

"In those days every man, woman and child who could run and use his hands was busy," Ellis claimed. "Work was the watchword! Industry the onward march! To this day it ever seems to me one of life's inspired lessons of faith, the Spirit hoping while hands were planting for the reward of toil."[2]

Although an education was difficult to obtain, Ellis had a great desire for knowledge. At school, she used quills for pens and slate slabs instead of paper. There were few books at home, but Ellis pored over what she had. She sewed large pockets in her dresses so that she could have a book handy when a few free minutes came her way. When she was just fourteen years old, she became a teaching assistant, helping the younger classes.

Ellis became acquainted with President Brigham Young, who was so impressed with the young girl that he invited her to come and live in Salt Lake City. That provided her with the opportunity to study under the tutelage of Karl G. Maeser, who later established Brigham Young Academy.

Ellis said of that time, "Those months I passed in the home of Brigham Young were for me very bright and profitable. . . . This home circle was the pattern of comfort, order and refinement, the abode of love, sweet peace and divine progression."[3]

She married Milford Shipp in 1866. During the next three years, she gave birth to three boys: Milford, William, and Richard. She lost one son, Willie, as a toddler. Her husband took two other wives, Margaret Curtis and Elizabeth, then was called on a mission to England. To support herself and her children while Milford was gone, Ellis did fancy sewing and taught school, while staying active in the Relief Society and Retrenchment organizations. She had to rise early each morning to accomplish everything.

"I have just completed my morning's work and have been resting about ten minutes, the longest respite I have had for weeks," Sister Shipp wrote one day. "With my school and the numerous other duties I have to perform, my time is completely monopolized."[4]

Ellis had poor health and was frustrated when it prevented her from accomplishing everything she wanted to do. She states, "I am still following out my plan of early rising and constant study whenever circumstances will permit—from four till seven will be my principal time . . . but if I am diligent I can accomplish something. How I long for knowledge and wisdom."[5]

Even when Milford returned home from his mission and relieved some of the financial burden, life was still difficult. He demanded quiet, which proved to be a challenge for three wives and many small children living together in a small house. Ellis' tender feelings were sometimes wounded when Milford seemed to have little time for her. Once she wrote, "The clouds look dark and my heart feels like it would break."[6] When life seemed hard, Ellis often turned to Brigham Young for personal counsel and he would give her comfort and support.

In April of 1873, she had a daughter, Anna. That August, Milford married Mary Smith Coteral. It was around this time that Eliza R. Snow, knowing of Ellis' interest in the subject, approached her with the idea of studying medicine. Sister

Snow reminded Ellis that it was Brigham's desire to see women educate themselves in this field.

"I thought it would be what I would love and delight in, if this knowledge could be obtained here," Sister Shipp said. "But the thought of leaving home and loved ones overwhelmed me and swept from me even the possibility of making the attempt."[7]

Ellis missed Milford who was frequently gone on missions, and when her beloved little Anna died, she became ill and despondent. Her fourth son, Burt Reynolds, was born in September of 1874 and the following spring, her health improved. She and Margaret began studying nursing with Dr. Washington F. Anderson. Over time, Ellis' aspiration to be a doctor grew. Finally, she told Milford of her dream and, to her joy, he encouraged her to pursue this goal. Margaret had also decided to become a doctor and was the first to leave for medical school. However, she became too homesick to continue and returned after four weeks.

Ellis worried about leaving her children. It seemed almost more than she could bear to leave the little ones that she loved more than life. But Mary, who had no children, promised that she would love and nurture Ellis' children as if they were her own. Another thing that troubled Ellis was her lack of a formal education—she had had almost no schooling. But when she sought out Brigham for counsel, he assured Ellis that she was well qualified and capable and encouraged her to go.

Sister Shipp left Salt Lake City on November 10, 1875, when her baby Burt was only fourteen-months-old. The pain of leaving her family was almost overwhelming.

She wrote, "Never will I forget this morning—nor the sadness upon the faces of my loved ones as I bade them goodbye. The parting is too painful to dwell upon. . . . My heart aches so sadly. . . ." Then she prayed, "Oh Heavenly Father, give me strength to endure the separation from my loved ones, and power to succeed in my endeavors to gain knowledge of medicine—that my life may be noble and useful upon the earth."[8]

Ellis arrived in Philadelphia and went to the Women's Medical College, a handsome four-story building. After paying her matriculation ticket of $5.00 and professor's fee of $45, classes began. As a new student, Ellis threw herself into her work, feeling an almost desperate need to succeed, not only for those whose lives she could save and the suffering she would alleviate, but for the sake of her husband and children whom she felt guilty at leaving. The strain of carrying such a heavy load showed. Ellis wrote in her journal:

"A lady remarked to me today, 'You always appear so sad, as though you were grieving over something.' I wonder if it is really true, if my countenance impresses all observers in this manner."[9]

Problems popped up. Disturbed by Ellis' habit of rising early, her landlord asked her to move. Then, since her new lodging didn't include meals, she had to spend time preparing her own food. Ellis tried to make up for the loss of time by being more organized, but was hampered when she began suffering from a pain in her side.

"This morning," Sister Shipp wrote, "I felt so sad and

lonely and the pain in my side seemed almost more than I could endure."[10]

In March of 1876, Ellis watched another class graduate from medical school. She struggled with her own feelings, as her remaining years of study seemed unbearably long. Still, she rejoiced in the learning.

"Began the study of blood, chemically. How interesting and delightful are my studies," Ellis wrote enthusiastically in her journal. "How happy must be a thoroughly educated person, for even the cursory knowledge I have gained in the last few months has opened to my view depths and heights of which I had never dreamed."[11]

When spring came, Milford came for a visit. Upon discovering that his wife was suffering from persistent side pains, he insisted she see a doctor who immediately sent Ellis to the hospital. Ellis said, "Both doctors advised me to return home and take a respite from my studies. They gave me medicines and told me to do all that I could to recruit my health."[12] One doctor told her that her heart was skipping beats and that she might not live more than six months. Milford asked his wife to come home to recuperate. When he assured her that she could return to school in the fall, Ellis packed her bags, even though she felt as though she was leaving her work undone.

Once home, Ellis exclaimed, "The happiest moments I ever experienced were this night when I clasped my darlings in my arms and prayed that we might nevermore be parted."[13]

Ellis was diligent in taking her medicine and was just recovering her health when she discovered that she was pregnant. Although she loved her unborn child fiercely, it seemed that her dream of becoming a doctor would be snatched away after all. She became despondent and asked for a blessing.

"Sister Ellis," Patriarch John Smith told her, "listen to the promptings of the Spirit and thy guardian angel shall whisper in thy ear and give thee counsel in time of need and strength in time of trial. Thy name shall be borne in honorable mention from generation to generation. . . . Thou shall have the gift of healing and be crowned with the mothers of Israel."[14]

Although Milford felt she ought to stay home, Ellis decided to return to Philadelphia, knowing she would have barely enough time to complete the school term before her baby was born. As Ellis made preparations to leave, she saw a notice in the newspaper about a group of Saints who were heading east on a special train. Here was her chance, she thought. Because the train was leaving the very next morning, Ellis had to work through the night, packing. Then one of her sons became ill with a sore throat and a high fever, making Ellis wonder if this was a sign that she was meant to stay home. As the sun peeked over the mountains, the worried mother went once more into her son's room. Smiling brightly, he told Ellis that he wasn't sick anymore. Her heart jumped. She could go after all.

After her return to medical school, finances became a great concern. Ellis barely had enough money to pay her fees. She lived on bread and milk, spending only fifty cents each week on groceries. She gave sewing lessons in exchange for food, which meant she had to do her studies late at night. In order to save on utility expenses, Sister Shipp spent long hours studying in the dissecting room or library, often staying until the janitor arrived to lock the doors. She spent all her holidays in the lab, even though it meant she had to do her weekly washing late at night. Her only recreation was writing letters.

Soon, her pregnancy became known and the doctors told her it would be impossible for her to continue. They felt it would be too much of a strain on her to attend classes, study her books, observe operations and dissect specimens. They said that performing all these tasks and other necessary work would surely harm her and her unborn child and suggested that she abort the child.

Ellis spent hours in prayer in her little attic room, praying for help, inspiration, and the strength to carry on. Sister Shipp then she went back to the doctors and told them she would not abort the baby— that she had come to learn how to save lives, not take them.

Even with her precarious health, Ellis did not miss a single session throughout that school year. The holidays dragged by and, when New Year's Day came, Sister Shipp had one dollar left to pay her bills. This meant she would have to sew more, which would entail missing some lectures. Worried about her finances, Ellis nevertheless trusted in the Lord. Then, one day the postman rang the doorbell. It was a letter from Elizabeth at home. Worried, Ellis tore it open. Inside was a money order for fifty dollars—an incredible sum of money. Tears flooded her face and her intense gratitude added to her already strong determination to succeed.

When winter term ended, Ellis found out that she had distinguished herself, passing anatomy, physiology, and chemistry with high marks. Although her professors praised her performance and determination, privately Ellis confessed that she didn't work hard in order to win praises.

"Heaven knows it is not for self I have thus absented myself from all that earth holds so dear. Tis not for worldly praise I labor early and late, but that I may become a more competent wife and mother and better qualified for all the duties of woman and of a Saint of God."[15]

By working feverishly, Ellis managed to complete her necessary class work before baby Olea appeared on May 25th. She hired a woman to care for her infant, then resumed her rounds through the hospital wards, diagnosing and prescribing. Afterwards, she would go home and stay up late at night washing, ironing, and studying. Ellis Reynolds Shipp finished up her final studies and graduated from the Women's Medical College of Pennsylvania on March 14, 1878.

Once back in Salt Lake City, the Women's Exponent carried an ad announcing that Dr. Ellis Shipp, the second woman doctor in Utah, would begin her practice and that her specialties were obstetrics, diseases of women, and minor surgery. Sister Shipp was set apart for her work and given a special priesthood blessing by Elder George Q. Cannon.

A conscientious mother, Ellis moved her children into better quarters right by her office. "I decided to live my life with every moment of my spare time given to my beloved children. I proceeded to move from the old home and established our family by our office rooms on Main Street. Thus began the happiest hours of my life. The blessed companionship of intelligent, forming, developing minds, the loving helpfulness of two noble sons whom God in his mercy had spared from the ravages of diphtheria to bless my life. If honors should ever come from the practice of my profession, my beloved sons should share them."[16]

Sister Shipp soon saw that there was a great need for competent medical care for women. She devised a plan to teach women the art of nursing and obstetrics and opened a medical school. Ellis wrote the examinations herself and had them approved by the Salt Lake City Board of Health. The following summer, her third daughter, Ellis, was born and in November, her son Burt died.

Dr. Shipp's practice became very busy and successful. Because she sought help from more experienced doctors when she had a question, the men came to have confidence in her. In fact, one doctor remarked to a patient, "You need have no fears when this woman is near, she knows her business."[17]

Dr. Shipp's services for women included prenatal care, delivery of the child, and ten visits after birth. During that time, she would bathe mother and child, make the bed, and even cook if necessary. She charged $25.00, but reduced it if the family could not afford it.

During her many years of practice, Sister Shipp brought more than six thousand babies into the world. She lost only one mother and that was a case where the family delayed in sending for a doctor. Ellis continued to read and study, wanting to provide her patients with the best and most up-to-date medical care available. She did post-graduate work and, whenever she traveled, went to local hospitals to observe new procedures.

She declared, "So long as I am a practitioner of the healing art I desire to keep pace with the onward move of this wonderful science of medicine."[18]

Ellis bore two more sons. One, Paul Elbert, lived only a few hours. The other, Ambrose Pare, lived only five months.

When Deseret Hospital opened, Ellis served voluntarily on a visiting basis and later became a member of the executive board. Using prayer as a tool for good and as a weapon against disease, she states, "I sought my Father and my God! He it was who inspired me with the higher intelligence, helped me to know my duty in all of its details, enabled me to run and not be weary, to walk and not faint."[19]

Besides participating in the Utah Woman's Press Club and serving on the Relief Society General Board, Ellis served as co-editor for *The Salt Lake City Sanitarian, a Monthly Journal of Medicine and Surgery*. She frequently contributed articles to the magazine. Then, in 1888, Ellis was chosen as one of those privileged to represent Utah at the International Council of Women in Washington D.C. In September, 1889, when Ellis was 42, her last child, Nellie, was born.

When the Deseret Hospital closed, the Relief Society organized a nursing school. Ellis began coordinating classes for women in outlying areas who could not come to the school. She began traveling a great deal throughout Mexico, Canada, and the Western United States, conducting classes in major cites.

"In 1899, I left with my Olea and my baby girl, Nellie for old Mexico. There we were received most kindly and I was soon very busy with a large class of fine women, teaching them the fundamentals of science, the subjects of nursing and obstetrics. Along with this I had daily and nightly calls."[20]

In 1910, a volume of Sister Shipp's poetry, *Life Lines,* was published. She dedicated the book of three hundred poems to her children.

As a fitting tribute to a remarkable pioneer doctor, Ellis was invited to the Women's Medical College in Philadelphia in 1935 to be honored as their oldest living graduate. Dean Martha Tracy gave Dr. Ellis Shipp the gold medal awarded to those graduates who had practiced medicine for over fifty years. As the medal was pinned on, the whole group gave Ellis a standing ovation.

"She had proven herself and come back with honors," writes Susan Evans McCloud. "The quiet little plural wife from Utah who had been told to go home and prepare to die, who had been advised to abort the child she carried, who had studied long hours alone in her attic room, defying both circumstances and tradition, stood before them now as a standard, a shining example of all that was best and noblest in their field, demonstrating the heights their profession could rise to when embraced by a woman of talent, dedication and integrity."[21]

Notes

1. Susan Evans McCloud, *Not In Vain,* (Salt Lake City: Bookcraft, 1984), p. 4.

2. Ellis Reynolds Shipp 1847–1939, *Autobiography [ca. 1930],* (Salt Lake City: LDS Church Archives), p. 12.

3. Ibid., p. 32.

4. *Early Autobiography and Diary of Dr. Ellis R. Shipp,* (Salt Lake City: LDS Church Archives), p. 47.

5. Ibid., p. 59.

6. Ibid., p. 65.

7. Ellis Reynolds Shipp 1847–1939, *Autobiography [ca. 1930],* op cit., p. iv.

8. *Early Autobiography and Diary of Dr. Ellis R. Shipp*, op cit., p. 142.

9. Ibid., p. 148.

10. Ibid., p. 149.

11. Ibid., p. 182.

12. Ibid., p. 194.

13. Ibid., p. 199.

14. Susan Evans McCloud, *Not In Vain*, op cit., p. 122.

15. *Early Autobiography and Diary of Dr. Ellis R. Shipp*, op cit., p. 210–211.

16. *Autobiography [ca. 1930],* (Salt Lake City: LDS Church Archives), p. 55.

17. Ibid., p. 53.

18. Ibid., p. 54.

19. Ibid.

20. Ibid., p. 55.

21. Susan Evans McCloud, *Not in Vain,* op cit., pp. 174–175.

Chapter 7

Elder Benjamin Brown & Elder Jesse Crosby

CONTINUING THROUGH TRIALS

It wasn't often that missionaries paddling a canoe down a river were invited to stop and speak about the gospel, but Elder Benjamin Brown and Elder Jesse W. Crosby were delighted to be asked. When the pair decided to go and tract in Nova Scotia, they bought a canoe. The elders were heading down St. John's River when they overtook a friendly man on a raft and struck up a conversation. The man was delighted to find out that they were preachers and invited them to stop at his house and hold a meeting on Sunday. Accepting the invitation happily, they rowed twenty miles down river to his house.

A large crowd gathered to listen to the missionaries on

that fine spring Sunday in 1844. Elder Crosby spoke first. Then Elder Brown bore his testimony. Afterwards, a family in the audience came up and invited the elders to dinner. The missionaries gladly accepted, but wondered momentarily why the mother was acting a little strangely. She seemed overly eager to have them come. When the meal was finished, the mother revealed why she had appeared so agitated earlier.

She confessed that ever since their previous minister had left the area, she had been praying for the Lord to send someone to teach them the gospel. The woman explained that she had recently had a vision in which two men spoke. The first one preached gospel doctrine. Then the other delivered a different type of speech, one with which she was unfamiliar.

The lady said that she distinctly remembered the clothing and appearance of the men in her vision. Yesterday, she had been very startled to see Elder Brown and Elder Crosby—for they were the men she had seen in her revelation. Then, when she heard Elder Crosby preach and Elder Brown bear his testimony—which was the "different type of speech" she had heard in her vision—she knew the two men were true messengers from God. Because of this spiritual manifestation, Elder Brown felt assured that the Lord was working in the area on their behalf.

"We commenced to baptize soon after the foregoing occurrence," he said, "and the Spirit of the Lord was mightily poured out, in proportion to which the powers of darkness began to manifest themselves through the unbelievers."[1]

It seemed that Satan could not bear to see the Church grow and so he called upon his evil followers to battle against the light. Enemies of the Church became enraged when some of the most important and influential men in the area were baptized. Spiteful men began to circulate all kinds of lies about the missionaries and Church doctrine. One claimed that the missionaries were in the habit of interrupting public meetings. Angry ministers sent a complaint against the Latter-day Saints to the Governor of New Brunswick. He, in turn, sent an order to three local justices of the peace, asking them to meet and establish evidence against the missionaries.

Most of the justices were bitter enemies of the Church and they searched the law books carefully to find something—anything—with which to accuse the elders. Eventually, they discovered an old statute that forbade all dissenters (i.e. those who did not accept the common religion) from holding public religious services without a written license from the governor. Because there were other religions in the area, this law had always been ignored. Nevertheless, the justices charged the missionaries with breaking this oft-violated but never— enforced law. The ultimate irony was that two of the justices were dissenters themselves who attended meetings where licenses had never been obtained.

When the day for the trial came, the missionaries found that the prosecutor had assembled all kinds of unsavory and unreliable witnesses. One witness was a man who had previously been convicted of lying under oath. It soon became clear that unless something happened, the prosecutors would convict the elders in spite of their innocence.

Elder Brown remarked, "I quickly discovered that it was high time to stir in the matter or possibly the next discovery would be that we were inmates of a jail."[2]

During a break in the trial, Squire Shelton, who had been recently baptized by the elders, advised them to go see Judge Bardsley, the county judge. Judge Bardsley had frequently attended the missionaries meetings and wrote a certificate stating that he had heard nothing in them that could be considered injurious to the people or the government. Elder Crosby and Elder Brown also obtained a similar certificate from Squire Shelton who was also a justice of the peace. Unfortunately, taking the two certificates to the governor proved to be a fruitless endeavor.

Elder Brown stated that the governor was "most terribly prejudiced against us and very ignorant of the law and gospel."[3] However, the governor's aid-de-camp was moved by their plight and listened to their story. When the aide saw that things were going badly for the missionaries, he stepped in and made an eloquent plea on their behalf. After two hours of arguing, the governor finally capitulated and ordered that the legal proceedings against the Mormons be stopped.

That decision enraged the enemies of the Church and dire threats were made against the missionaries. Fearful for their lives, the elders began sleeping in the woods. They were forced to perform their baptisms at night to prevent mobs from disrupting the services.

One day, a foe of the Church overheard Elder Brown promise to visit an investigator the next day. He quickly alerted his friends. The next day, ten men hid alongside the road, waiting to ambush the unsuspecting young man. As Elder Brown walked by, they jumped out of the brush and knocked him to the ground. Several men held the defenseless missionary down while others beat him. One man took off Elder Brown's boot and struck his head repeatedly with the heel until blood ran freely down onto the ground. Then, they grabbed hold of the missionary's hands and feet and raised him off the ground before throwing him down violently. Several jumped on top of him with their knees, breaking his ribs. Elder Brown fought back but was woefully outnumbered. Suddenly, it occurred to him that if he feigned death, the mob might leave.

He relates, "So I groaned loudly as if dying and resigned myself into their hands, holding my breath as much as possible,"[4] he said. His ruse succeeded, partly because of the darkness. Believing they had accomplished their goal, the mob dispersed. After his attackers left, Elder Brown rose stiffly and stumbled to Squire Shelton's house where Elder Crosby administered to him.

It didn't take long for the mob to find out that Elder Brown was not dead. They made plans to finish the job that very night and to kill Elder Crosby as well. It was discovered later that their grisly plan included cutting off Elder Crosby's ears, tarring and feathering both of the elders, then carrying them out to the middle of St. John's River where they intended to tie stones around their feet and toss them into the river. The missionaries had no inkling of the mob's plans until late that night when a wooden rail was hurled through the window. It landed on top of the elders as they lay asleep in their beds.

Then, the mobbers broke into Squire Shelton's house and

several of them began banging away at the missionaries' locked bedroom door, trying to break it down. They would have burst through but Mrs. Shelton became alarmed at the noise and, carrying a lighted candle, came to investigate. Fearful of being recognized, the men ran off, shouting loudly to warn those in other parts of the house. After the men had gone, Squire Shelton decided to alert his neighbors in case the mob decided to come back. His hunch was correct—the mob's retreat was only temporary.

Elder Brown stated that the mob returned while the squire was still gone, having "recruited their spirits with whiskey." On their second attack, they attempted to enter their room by a different door but had a difficult time because, "Elder Crosby held the door with an iron grasp and the resolution of a lion."[5]

One man did manage to get an arm through but just as he did, was grabbed around his ample waist by Squire Shelton's strong son. The son, who lived on a nearby farm, had been awakened by his father and had raced over to help. Shortly after, the squire arrived with additional help. When Squire Shelton recognized several members of the mob, he put them under bonds. Angrily, the mobbers threatened to burn down his house and barn if he prosecuted them. Soberly, the squire realized that the government, disliking the Latter-day Saints as they did, would never sanction a conviction, even with witnesses and all his evidence. Unhappily, he decided to let them go.

Elder Brown wrote, "The next day, by the blessing of God, I recovered sufficiently to walk seventeen miles and preach, but my face was discolored, and I could only see with one eye.

I took for my text Paul's words: 'Thrice have I been beaten with stripes,' etc." He went on, "My personal appearance furnished a very favorable evidence on behalf of my argument that the same effects, violence and death, followed the preaching of the Gospel in these days as it did anciently."

Despite continued threats, the missionaries continued to spread the news of the restored gospel. Elder Brown affirmed, "Not withstanding the above, we did not leave the country but continued to preach, fearless of opposition, until we had baptized about 50, out of which we organized two branches. These were also visited abundantly with the signs following and the Saints rejoiced greatly in the work. The persecution was a failure in Satan's calculation, it only excited curiosity and awakened attention."[6]

Notes

1. Benjamin Brown, *Testimonies For The Truth*, (London: S. W. Richards, 1853), p. 21.

2. Ibid., p. 22.

3. Ibid.

4. Ibid.

5. Ibid., p. 23.

6. Ibid.

Chapter 8

James S. Brown

THE AMERICAN PLANT

In the fall of 1849, Elder James S. Brown was called to go on a mission to the Society Islands. Before he left, President Willard Richards gave him a prophetic blessing. He told James that, while he was on his mission, men would seek his life and at times it would appear like he could not possibly escape, yet angels would draw near and deliver him from harm. This special blessing was to be fulfilled more literally than Elder Brown ever thought possible.

On May 24th, 1850, Elder Brown arrived at Papeete, the capital of Tahiti. He was dismayed when authorities refused to give him permission to preach. Ministers of other religions had used their considerable influence with the French government—who ruled the islands—in order to deny the Latter-day Saint missionaries the right to proselyte. The governor even refused to let them visit the nearby island of Tubuai.

When the missionaries protested, the governor asked them to furnish a detailed statement of their principles, methods, and pledges. They did, but were still forbidden to travel to any of the islands. While the elders continued their efforts to change the governor's mind, they spent their free time learning the language. The local people were very surprised at their quick progress. One native stated that the Lord had to be with the Latter-day Saints because in five months, they spoke the language better than other foreigners did after spending five years there.

After many months, the elders finally received permission to go about their labors. Elder Brown visited various islands and in December, arrived at Raivavai, a small island about fourteen miles in circumference. Of the 383 people who lived on the island, just eight were members of the Church.

At first, Elder Brown spent his time visiting each house, doing his best to be friendly and sociable with the people. He then asked for permission to preach and did so with some success, although a few were suspicious of him and his "new" religion. Misgivings escalated when several converts were baptized. Some of the tribal leaders became so upset and angry that they held a council to determine how to get rid of Mormonism and the "American Plant," as they called Elder Brown.

James wrote, "Some proposed to fasten the "plant" on a log, tow it out to sea, where the sharks would eat it, while others suggested burning or making a roast of me."[1] At last, the agitated council decided to give the missionary two options—either leave the island or be killed. Word about the verdict quickly spread. When Elder Brown was told about the decision, he went quickly to the council to assuage their fears about his religion and to persuade them to change their minds.

Unfortunately, he said, "I found it utterly impossible to reason with them. My presence, instead of having a conciliatory effect, created the wildest confusion."

As James tried to pacify them, a stout, heavy-set man named Tabate became enraged and charged the missionary, shouting, "I will slay you!"[2] Friends restrained Tabate, allowing Elder Brown to leave.

Eventually, the council decided not to take any action at that time. Although bitter feelings remained among some of the people, Elder Brown continued his labors, blessing infants and administering to the sick. Many people were miraculously healed of their ailments after receiving blessings at his hands. He was also able to baptize twenty new members.

From time to time, councils were held to decide what could be done about getting rid of the "American Plant," as some still called him. But there were now many converts, who—along with their friends and relatives—were opposed to taking any harsh actions against the elder.

However, hostile feelings were magnified when an important chief requested that his granddaughter, heir to the throne, be baptized. Some of the people were convinced that she had been beguiled and misled. In order to soothe the angry natives, the chief called for a meeting. There, the young girl, Teraa, declared to the crowd that it was her own desire to become a member of the Church and that Elder Brown had not unduly influenced her. Her declaration helped calm the people.

For a time, there was comparative quiet. Then, false rumors and slander about the Church began circulating once more. Matters took a distinct turn for the worse when two young ministers of another faith came to the island and made inflammatory speeches. The ministers told the natives that they had admitted a wolf into their fold and declared that if the people didn't get rid of Elder Brown, they would not return to the island. Since the ministers were widely liked and respected, the natives were very disturbed at this declaration.

The ministers urged, "Drive him [Elder Brown] off and pluck up that American Plant, or it will overshadow your land and control you."

Elder Brown said of that time, "Now everyone was sad and gloomy. The spirit of mobocracy seemed to thrive on the islanders. Meetings were held and threats were made. Clouds of darkness lowered and filled the atmosphere; the spirit of death seemed to hover around, for the boisterousness of the people had given way to a sullen, murderous disposition, more to be dreaded than when there was abundance of noise and threats."[3]

Matters came to a head on May 5, 1852, when the natives held a great council at the village of Tatake. Everyone came for the feast and to hear the chief's final decision on what would happen with the Mormon minister. People gathered to the village, laden down with roast pig, fruit, fish, and poultry. As the council convened, the people began singing, dancing, eating, and arguing. Meanwhile, all the worried Saints on Raivavai gathered into one small building for safety.

Outside the small hut, brash young men danced around, shouting. In their excitement, a mob tore down the fence that surrounded the house and made a bonfire. Then they made a lime kiln and covered it with coral rock. All night, the Saints could hear the firing of guns and the chanting of war songs. No one could sleep, so they held a fast and testimony meeting, which lasted all night.

About 1:00 P.M., two large men with clubs came to collect Elder Brown and take him to the council. They had been told to drag him if he refused. As Elder Brown rose, he recalled the promise that President Brigham Young had given him prior to his departure:

"He told me, in the name of the Lord God of Israel, that though men should seek my life, yet I should return in safety, having done good and honor to myself and the Church and the Kingdom of God."[4]

Remembering the Prophet's words, as well as Elder Richard's blessing, helped Elder Brown stay calm. He turned to his guards with no more fears or doubts. The crowd watched curiously as he walked confidently to the assembly of chiefs and stood before them strong and tall. Those he had converted followed in his footsteps. To his left burned the huge bonfire. Nearby, stood fifteen young, athletic natives clad only in loincloths. Their brown bodies glistened as they watched in sober silence.

Tabate stepped forward and fiercely ordered, "All the Britons stand on the right hand with the sheep and the

Mormons stand on the left where the goats are." Two faithful Church members, Rivae and his wife who was carrying an eight-month-old baby in her arms, stepped forward. They knew what Tabate had planned.

"If you burn this man," Rivae boldly announced, pointing at Elder Brown, "you must burn me first."

His wife also spoke up. "I am a Mormon and this baby will be a Mormon if he lives, so you will have to burn all of us to put a stop to Mormonism." Tabate ordered them to stand aside. He then turned his attention back to the missionary, accusing him of leading the people astray.

Elder Brown opened his Bible. "Show me where the teaching is wrong from the Bible." One of the chiefs told him to shut the book, that the decision had already been made to burn him to death.

In an exultant voice, Tabate pointed at the fire. "Look there at that fire. It is made to consume the flesh off of your bones." Elder Brown looked, but instead of being overcome with fear was filled with the Holy Spirit. Later James said he felt as though he could run through a troop.

"In the name of Israel's God," he declared, raising his arms high in the air, "I defy the host of you, for I serve that God who delivered Daniel from the den of lions and the three Hebrew children from the fiery furnace!"[5]

The people stood in open-mouthed awe at the missionary's unshaken confidence. There was not one particle of fear in his whole being and, while many of the people shouted that someone should throw him into the fire, no one dared make a move to touch him. Then, his opponents began quarreling and fighting among themselves. Finally, the crowd dispersed, everyone going their own way. The bonfire was left to burn itself out. In the days following the meeting, a feeling of quiet and safety pervaded the village—a peaceful feeling that had not been there for many weeks.

Months later, Elder Brown was walking down a path when he noticed that ahead of him was one of the men who had wanted to kill him. When the older man happened to turn around and see the missionary, he suddenly took off running. Curious, Elder Brown sprinted after him. Managing to catch up with the native, Elder Brown grabbed his arm and pulled him to a stop.

Breathlessly he asked, "Why do you run from me?"

"Your God is a God of power and I was afraid to meet his servant," the man admitted. He then went on to tell Elder Brown of an unusual manifestation he had seen on that fateful night.

He said, "At the moment that you defied us, there was a brilliant light, or pillar of fire, bore down close over your head. We thought you had prayed to your God and that he had sent that fire to burn us and our people if we harmed you. The young men did not see the light. They were going to burn you and we tried to stop them. So we got into a fight. Now we all know that you are a true servant of God, and we do not like to meet you, out of fear."

Startled at first, Elder Brown reassured the man that he meant no harm and wanted only to share the good news of the gospel. "I was treated with great respect ever afterwards,"

Elder Brown related. "Indeed there never was another council meeting called to devise a way to get rid of the Mormons from that island while I remained there. . . . A feeling of quiet and safety pervaded the village, especially in and about our residence, such as we had not before known on the island."[6]

Notes

1. James S. Brown, *Life Of A Pioneer; Being The Autobiography of James S. Brown*, (Salt Lake City: George Q. Cannon and Sons Company, 1900), p. 240.

2. Ibid., pp. 240–241.

3. Ibid., p. 244.

4. Ibid., p. 247.

5. Ibid., pp. 277–248.

6. Ibid., pp. 251–252.

Chapter 9

John Alexander
TWELVE STEPS

John Alexander sang heartily as he swung along the dirt road. The year was 1883 and he was returning from preaching in the nearby city of Adairsville, Georgia. Most of the morning had been spent talking to farmers and he was now returning to Brother Reed's home where he was staying.

Walking along briskly in the morning sunshine, Elder Alexander was startled when three masked men jumped out of the brush, blocking his path. Their faces were hidden by large squares of unbleached calico, which had been tied around their heads and hung down to the middle of their chests. Their hats were pulled down so low over their foreheads that only their narrowed eyes showed.

A lean man, over six feet tall, was the apparent leader. He asked gruffly, "Are you one of those Mormon elders from

Utah?" When the missionary confirmed that he was, the masked man nodded toward the hill. "You go up there in the brush."

Thoroughly alarmed, Elder Alexander blurted out, "I don't feel like going up. What do you want me to go for?"

"You go," the mobster demanded angrily. "I won't tell you again."[1] To back up his terse words, he drew out his pistol and pointed it at the missionary. The two other men did the same. With three guns trained on him, there was nothing else for Elder Alexander to do but follow as one of the men led the way up the tree-covered hill. The other two followed close behind.

When the missionary had walked fifty yards into the brush, he stopped and turned around. The leader brusquely told him to go on, but Elder Alexander replied that he had gone as far as he was going to. Infuriated, the men again drew their pistols and pointed them at the missionary. Frustrated and helpless to do anything other than obey, he turned and again started up the hill. Just then, one of the men unexpectedly kicked him viciously from behind, hurling him forward on his hands and knees.

Quickly, Elder Alexander raised himself and swung wildly at his attacker who was down the slope from him. He missed, struck a small tree instead and fell flat on the ground. That prompted the leader to charge. When Elder Alexander rolled over, the leader jumped on him and the third mobster began kicking him in his left side. Then the assailants backed off, allowing the missionary to get slowly to his feet. They signaled him to continue climbing. Trying not to moan, Elder Alexander limped about a hundred and fifty yards, clutching his stomach, then stopped again. Facing the masked men, he spread his hands apart.

"For God's sake, men, you don't mean to kill a young, innocent man. What have I done?"

"Well," the leader answered, "you came out here preaching false doctrine and you know it's false and say that it is."

"No sir," the shocked elder exclaimed. "I don't think it's false; I know it is not false and I can't say that it is."

"Well, you're going to die right here," the leader announced. "Have you anything to say?" Elder Alexander replied that if they truly meant to kill him, he did indeed have something to say."Well, what is it?"

"Will you allow me to offer up a few words of prayer?"

"Yes," the leader consented. "If you'll be quick about it."

Holding up his right hand, Elder Alexander placed his left hand across his chest. "Oh, my God, if it is thy will that these men should take my life, I am willing to die."[2] He murmured a few more words before folding his arms against his chest. Lifting his head, he stared directly at the hooded men with raised pistols. Elder Alexander saw the leader aim at his face. The other man pointed slightly lower. The missionary took a quick breath and closed his eyes. Three shots rang out. He felt himself falling and lost consciousness.

When Elder Alexander came to, he was on his hands and knees, blearily staring at the ground with bowed head. Shakily, he got to his feet and staggered over the ground until he reached the road. Dazed, the missionary had no thoughts of where he should go for help, only that he needed to keep moving. Finally, Elder Alexander found himself at a fence. Just as he looked around and realized it was near Brother Reed's home, he stumbled and fell to the ground. Brother Reed happened to be working outside and saw him fall. Hurrying over, he picked up the missionary and carried him into the house.

The family gathered round as Brother Reed removed the elder's coat, sponged his face and made him as comfortable as he could. Half an hour later, Elder Alexander had regained his senses enough so that he could speak. He related his chilling experience. Then he asked for his hat and coat.

Holding the black and white straw hat in his hand, Elder Alexander recalled that he had been standing a bit above the mobsters on the hill. His hat had been tilted back slightly on his head. Gingerly, he touched the circular holes in the straw hat that one bullet had made. It had gone through the front of the hat, then inexplicably turned up immediately, exiting at the crown.

Elder Alexander knew that particular shot had been fired by the leader, for just before he had closed his eyes, he had seen the leader point his pistol directly at his head.

Next, the missionary examined his coat. While standing on the hill, his coat had fallen open slightly. The second shot had passed through the coat on his left side, just grazing the side of his watch chain. Somehow, the third ball had missed him completely.

Elder Alexander looked up at the Reed family, clustered around him. All of them were staring in shock at the holes in his clothing. The look of wondering awe he saw on their faces was reflected on his own, for he knew that when the mobsters had fired, they had been standing only twelve steps away.

Notes

1. "Our Injured Missionary," *Juvenile Instructor, Vol. 18*; 1883, p. 207.
2. Ibid.

Chapter 10

Claudius V. Spencer

MORMON IMPUDENCE

In the early years of the Church, men were often called to go on missions during general conference, without having any advance notice or warning. Claudius V. Spencer had a premonition one Sunday that he might be called on a mission during that general conference and so stayed away, working on the hopeful premise that if he was out of sight, he would also be out of mind. As the minutes ticked by, however, curiosity got the best of him. When the meeting was close to ending, Claudius walked to the tabernacle and cautiously opened the outer door a few inches to listen. Just then, a man at the podium made an announcement.

"It is moved and seconded that Claudius V. Spencer go on a mission to Europe." Stricken, Claudius stumbled backwards. He wondered, "Can it be possible those men have any inspiration to call such a stick for a missionary?"[1]

Having never before spoken—or even prayed—in public, Claudius had great doubts about his abilities. However, such misgivings were not shared by God or by the leaders of the Church. Indeed, when Claudius was set apart, Heber C. Kimball declared that he would be like Paul of old in the land to which he was going.

In the company of other departing elders, Elder Spencer left Salt Lake City on the 19th of April 1850. He literally went without purse or scrip, taking no watch, ring, money or anything of value. On their first day of travel, the company was hit by a storm which scattered their cattle. It took days of hard work to round them up. They continued on, with the incredibly deep snow making travel very difficult.

"We would frequently sink into the snow almost to our necks," Claudius said, "and after crawling out, the sun would melt the snow on our clothes so that at night we were as wet as though we had been immersed in water. In the mornings we stood on the snow crusts, beat our boots and pantaloons over the wagon wheels to get the ice out of them before we could dress."[2]

Along the way, the company was stricken with cholera and Claudius was among those who fell ill. One evening, just as they began to turn off the main road to go down to the Platte River to cook their supper, Elder Spencer frantically asked them to stop. Remembering the blessing he had received at the hand of President Kimball, the literal-minded Claudius begged his companions not to take him off the main road, for he had been promised that he should not die "on the road to England."

Elder Spencer told the perplexed missionaries that they could go ahead and prepare their meal at the river as they had planned, only if they would take him out of the wagon and lay him on the ground first—facing England. Elder Spencer warned them that if they returned to find him dead, they had better return home, for his demise would prove that Mormonism was a hoax. However, Claudius was alive when they returned and eventually made a full recovery.

As the missionaries continued across the country, elders began departing, bound for various destinations within the United States, and Elder Spencer was alone when he reached the eastern states. After boarding a ship for New York, Satan began preying upon him and Claudius became depressed, feeling that the authorities had made a colossal mistake by calling him on a mission when he was such a inexperienced speaker.

As he was darkly reflecting upon these and other gloomy thoughts, a fellow traveler struck up a conversation with him. But Elder Spencer was in no mood to respond, even when the man exhibited an interest in Salt Lake City and the Church. In an effort to get rid of his unwelcome companion, Claudius was deliberately rude but the man shrugged off his impolite behavior. Elder Spencer couldn't believe it when his jovial acquaintance actually invited him to dine with his group. Morosely, he declined. Later, he was approached by the same man who—showing no end of persistence—had brought a group of friends with him, hoping that their numbers would cause the reluctant missionary to change his mind about dinner. Claudius refused again and was shocked and dismayed when the group informed him that they had procured an empty cabin and wanted him to preach that very night.

Aghast, Elder Spencer exclaimed, "I have never preached in my life!"

Thoroughly bewildered, one man responded, "Why then are you going to England?"

"To preach."

"Why then won't you preach here?"

Obstinately he replied, "I wasn't sent *here* to preach."[3]

However, by persevering, they finally wore Claudius down enough so that he agreed to answer a few questions. The group was so large, that when they packed themselves into the cabin, no one could sit down. The session went very well and continued until 11 P.M. The people were so pleased that they offered Elder Spencer three hundred dollars. He refused to accept the money, explaining that he had enough to get to England, but did ask three honorable men to take the money and give it to the poor. After the crowd left, Elder Spencer prostrated himself on the floor, thanking God for the gift of the Holy Ghost and asking forgiveness for his unbelief.

Upon arriving in New York City, he joined other missionaries and sailed to England, paying ten dollars for his passage. Apostle Orson Pratt, who was President of the British Mission, met Claudius in Liverpool. He was then sent on to London, which was known as a difficult place to win converts.

"It was a hard place," Elder Spencer stated, then drolly

added, "and in order to have raised any life there in relation to 'Mormonism,' one would have required the power to resurrect the dead."[4]

One day, Claudius set out for a town twenty miles distant. It was a hard walk, as the roads were wet and his carpetbag heavy. He was within sight of the town when he saw a woman in front of him begin to cross the road. When the woman turned and caught sight of him, she dropped the pails she was carrying with a clatter.

Running over, she exclaimed, "I knew you would come; I saw you in a dream. Come into my house; I have a room all fixed nice and clean for you." Elder Spencer performed his first baptisms in that village and soon after was named to the presidency of the Norwich Conference. Still, he harbored great doubts about his leadership abilities.

"I do not think any man ever entered upon the discharge of his duties as president with more distrust than I did," Claudius related. "And I wish to record here that the great good accomplished was God's work, for He worked through me; I only knew enough to speak and act as directed by the Holy Spirit. . . . For months afterwards people would say to me, when the meeting was over, 'I heard your knees knock together when you first began to speak.'"[5]

One time, Elder Spencer felt impressed to go to a certain town to preach. On the way, he stopped to meet with the local branch president and elders. When he told them about his plans, they were vehemently opposed, and told him they had met with intense persecution in that particular area. However, Elder Spencer said he would not change his plans.

Finally, the president warned him, saying, "Brother Spencer, if you go to that place, I clear myself of the consequences, your blood be upon your own head."

Elder Spencer had a quick retort. "If my blood be shed, it will be upon the heads of those who shed it, and those who ought to have, but have not got faith to sustain me."[6] He then asked for volunteers to accompany him. After much hesitation, the youngest elder present agreed to go.

After walking thirty-seven miles to reach the city, Elder Spencer asked permission to speak in the lone building on the common. He then went with the young elder from house to house, notifying people of the meeting. Soon, they were being followed by a crowd of children who jeered and threw sticks, stones and other objects. Tired of the harassment, Elder Spencer's young companion suddenly disappeared.

It was dusk when Claudius wearily arrived at the meeting place. He was pleased to see the building full and people milling about outside. However, Elder Spencer soon discovered the general attitude of the people toward Mormons when someone greeted him by hitting him on the head with a clump of sod. It was a hefty piece and thrown so hard that it knocked him to the ground. Picking dirt out of his ear, Claudius prayed briefly. He rose, then stretching out both hands in front of him as if he were about to dive, made a rush for the crowd, which parted enough to allow him to enter the building.

Once inside, Claudius went straight to the pulpit and quoted the first scripture that came to his head. He then waited for inspiration on what to say next. When several minutes had passed without any message being put into his mind, he began to worry. Then an idea hit him. He called the audience's attention to his pitiful condition, noting that he was among strangers and thousands of miles away from home. He continued to enumerate his afflictions and pathetic circumstances.

"In a few moments," he said, "several handkerchiefs were out, wiping tearful eyes. I had a glorious meeting."[7]

Just as he was finishing, a minister stood and began to disparage him over certain points of doctrine. But Claudius had thoroughly won the crowd over to his side. Unhappy with how the minister was rebuking the pitiable missionary, the crowd hoisted the unfortunate pastor above their shoulders and carried him and his complaints out of the building. Three men then took Elder Spencer to the best inn in town and paid the bill. During his stay in the village, he was able to baptize sixteen people.

Once during his mission, Elder Spencer hired a town hall to hold a meeting. After advertising around town, he stated that much more interest had been created than he felt good about. Anxiously, he acknowledged, "As the importance of the meeting grew, so also grew a sense of my own littleness and I sent word to Elder G. B. Wallace and Elder Harmon to come and help me."[8] To make sure that his intended speakers showed up, the apprehensive missionary even sent them money to pay their way.

On the day of the meeting, he heard that a mob planned to attend. The news worried him, but since the money to rent the hall had already been paid, Claudius was determined to see the meeting through. After the opening prayer, he called on

Brother Harmon to speak and was dumbfounded when the man returned to his seat after talking just two minutes. Then it was Brother Wallace's turn. When that good man's oration lasted a mere ninety seconds, Claudius frowned, feeling that he had hardly gotten his money's worth. He was at a complete loss at what to do as he listened to the peevish crowd murmuring unpleasantly.

After praying mightily for inspiration, Elder Spencer stood up and told them he was going to sing a comic song. Entranced at this novelty, the crowd gave him a cheer. When he was done warming up the audience, Claudius began to speak about more solemn matters.

"I continued speaking for one hour, and from the first five minutes the dropping of a pin on the floor could have been heard."[9] His sermon was a tremendous success and Elder Spencer decided that never again would he ask others to take his place at preaching.

Some time later, he went with Elder Wallace to a country branch. They quietly notified the people that an American gentleman would lecture that evening. Because the area was well-known for its virulent opposition to missionaries, Elder Spencer came up with a unique way to quiet the outbursts that were common at such gatherings.

Just before the meeting, Claudius hurriedly changed into a set of clothes he had previously acquired, hoping no one would recognize him in his disguise. At the appointed hour, he went to a corner near where the meeting would be held. He waited until the Church was almost full before approaching the door. When the meeting was about to begin, Elder

Spencer sauntered in and stood at the back, wearing the spotless uniform of a policeman. Surveying the people haughtily, he gave a splendid imitation of a person in authority, making himself as visible as possible, so that anyone who had planned to disturb the meeting would think twice before doing so.

When Elder Wallace took the stand, his camouflaged companion thrust out his chest and strolled pompously around the back of the building, a fine figure of law and order. All was quiet and Elder Wallace was allowed to preach his sermon. Many would-be dissenters were quieted by the sight of the club that dangled from Elder Spencer's hand, a weapon which he occasionally twirled for a more dramatic effect. The disguised missionary kept his place against the inside of the door and, as occasion warranted, went up the aisle to tap men on the shoulder if their mutterings grew too loud or if they acted disruptive in any way. His authority was never questioned and he was successful at keeping the peace—at least until the meeting was over.

After the last "amen," Elder Wallace quickly made for the back door. As people began leaving, Claudius knew his chances of being recognized would be greatly increased, since people would now be able to view his face directly. Knowing he would be in danger if anyone identified him, Elder Spencer managed to push his way out the front door. But it was too late. Someone in the crowd spotted him and shouted out the deception. In the ensuing melee, the doors were locked. The furious mob, thinking the missionaries were still inside, milled around the front of the building, shouting out dire threats.

However, the missionaries were able to leave through a back door and laughed as they made their way to their lodging.

For the next two weeks, the newspapers overflowed with accounts of Elder Spencer's 'Mormon impudence' by dressing up as a policeman. However, such publicity worked to the missionaries' advantage and dramatically increased the number of curious investigators at their meetings.

"In a little while we could not call a meeting anywhere in the conference but what it would be crowded," Elder Spencer declared. "Curiosity was above par."[10]

Although he faced continual threats and the hands of many were set against him, Elder Spencer continued to hold meetings, going forth boldly doing the Lord's work.

Another one of his adventurous meetings occurred in Norwich. When a friend idly mentioned that there was going to be a big anti-Mormon meeting in St. Andrew's Hall, Elder Spencer brightened as if he had been personally invited.

"Very well," he said happily. "I will brush up and go to it."[11] Appalled at the very idea, the other elders pleaded with him not to go but he was determined. Upon entering the huge hall, Claudius found it so packed—with over two thousand in attendance—that he couldn't find an empty seat. Then, looking up toward the stand, he saw seventeen ministers seated, with only a few vacant seats around them that were being saved for members of the clergy.

"I also am a minister," he thought to himself, "and that is my place." Walking boldly past the crowds, he took a seat among the other preachers. For the next five hours, he listened to speakers who were soundly critical of the Latter-day Saints and their doctrine.

Finally, the chairman announced that "if any member of the unfortunate 'Mormon Church' was present, who had the hardihood and moral courage to attempt a defense after such an overwhelming exposure of their system as has been made this day to the citizens of Norwich, he would be allowed to speak."[12]

When Elder Spencer rose, all eyes turned to him, but he was five rows behind the pulpit and quite unable to reach it. The rows were crammed with opponents, none of whom offered to draw up their knees and let him pass. After praying briefly, he put his hands on the heads of the two ministers in front of him, pushed outward to make an opening and lunged forward. He did this again with the next row and the next until he finally reached the pulpit. He then began speaking with great vigor.

At times, the Spirit was so strong within him that he was not fully aware of his own words and later asked others what he had said. When he was finished, the chairman tried to make a rebuttal by reading from the Book of Mormon but, inexplicably, the poor man began trembling so badly that it was impossible for him to read. Another man took up the book, intent on attacking it, but was affected the same way and could not continue.

Despite his powerful talk and these manifestations, Elder Spencer knew the feelings of the crowd were dark and angry and that they were close to violence. As soon as the meeting was dismissed, Elder Spencer hurried to a stairway, hoping to make a quick escape. Unfortunately, the stairs were crowded with people clamoring for his capture.

"Where is he?" one cried.

"Tear him from limb to limb!" another shouted.

"Throw him into the river!"[13] a man angrily shouted.

As Elder Spencer struggled to get through the nearly impenetrable mob, he feared escape would be impossible. Suddenly, a tall man wearing a large, billowing cloak slipped alongside him. Throwing one side of his cloak up and outward, the stranger took a step closer and, as the cloak fell, it covered the missionary to his shins.

"Be still," the man whispered, "and I will save you."[14] The stranger then moved outside, along with Elder Spencer who crouched low so that he remained hidden from view. As the mob surged forward, searching for the escaped Mormon missionary, they swept Claudius and his benefactor along with them down the road.

They had gone some distance when the deliverer reached his own home. Using his fist, the man struck the spring of a door set in the stone wall, causing it to fly open. Quickly, he tossed Elder Spencer into the yard, as if he were a log of wood. The door closed instantly and the stranger proceeded on with the unsuspecting crowd. After some time had passed, the man returned with friends who guarded the elder as they walked him home.

During his mission, people occasionally gave Elder Spencer money but he used all of it to help the poor and the sick. When the time came for him to return home, he didn't even have five shillings saved toward his fare. However, at the last possible moment, Claudius was presented with a large sum of money and used part of it to buy his passage home. When he arrived in Salt Lake City, Elder Spencer took the two hundred and seventy-five dollars he had left and presented the money to President Brigham Young with the humble request that it be sent to the poor in the Norwich Conference.

"Brother Spencer," President Young replied, "you are the first returned missionary that ever did the like."[15] Although Claudius had been consumed with doubts when first called to be a missionary, he fulfilled his errand from the Lord heroically.

Notes

1. *Labors In The Vineyard, Twelfth Book of the Faith Promoting Series*, (Salt Lake City: Juvenile Instructor Office, 1884), p. 9.

2. Ibid., p. 10.

3. Ibid., p. 14.

4. Ibid., p. 15.

5. Ibid., pp. 16–17.

6. Ibid., p. 18.

7. Ibid., p. 19.

8. Ibid., p. 20.

9. Ibid., p. 21.

10. Ibid., p.22.

11. Ibid., p. 23.

12. Ibid., p. 23.

13. Ibid.

14. Ibid., p. 25.

15. Ibid., p. 26.

Chapter 11

Wilford Woodruff

Listening To The Still Small Voice

During Church services that were held on the evening of his birthday, March 1, 1840, Elder Wilford Woodruff felt the Lord speak, saying; "This is the last meeting that you will hold with this people for many days."[1] He was surprised because he had already set many appointments in that fruitful missionary district of Hanley, England, and felt he could gain many converts. However, when Brother Woodruff prayed the next morning to receive further instructions, he was told to go south, that many souls were waiting and that the Lord had a great work for him to perform there.

No elder of The Church of Jesus Christ had ever visited that particular area before, but the next day, Wilford obediently took a coach and late that evening arrived at Ledbury, Herefordshire. Exhausted after traveling forty-eight miles by coach and on foot, he met Mr. and Mrs. John Benbow, a well-to-do couple who owned over three-hundred acres and had great influence in the area.

"I found Mr. Benbow to be a wealthy farmer," stated Wilford. "I presented myself to him a missionary from America, an elder of The Church of Jesus Christ of Latter-day Saints who has been sent to preach the gospel of life. He and his wife received me with glad hearts and thanksgiving."[2]

He was invited to stay for dinner. Afterwards, they began discussing the gospel. The couple was so curious about the idea of the true Church of Christ being restored to earth, that they stayed up until 2 A.M. Mr. Benbow told Elder Woodruff that there was a large group of people living nearby who had broken off from the Wesleyan Methodist sect and were called the United Brethren. He felt that they would like to hear about the Church of Jesus Christ. According to Mr. Benbow, the United Brethren were continually calling upon the Lord to open the way and send them light, truth, and knowledge. They had a great desire to know the true way to be saved.

"I rejoiced greatly at the news Mr. Benbow gave me," Elder Woodruff said, "that there was a company of men and women —over six hundred in number who had broken off from the Wesleyan Methodists and taken the name of United Brethren. I could clearly see why the Lord had commanded me to go to the South; for in Herefordshire there was a great harvest-field for gathering many saints into the kingdom of God."[3]

To comply with the law in England at that time, it was necessary to preach in a building that was specifically licensed for preaching. Fortunately, Mr. Benbow had a large hall in his mansion that was licensed. He sent word throughout the countryside that an American missionary would preach that evening at his house. The meeting was a great success and Elder Woodruff held another one the following evening. He later baptized six people, including the Benbows and four preachers of the United Brethren.

He spent the next day working hard, shoveling out a pool of water so he could use it for the many baptisms he was anticipating. As the weeks passed, the pool *was* used frequently, as Elder Woodruff ended up baptizing approximately six hundred people from the United Brethren.

On Sunday, March 8th, Elder Woodruff was gratified to hold three well-attended meetings. However, others were not so pleased with his success. One of the disgruntled onlookers was the preacher of the nearby parish Church who was greatly alarmed by his shrinking congregation. On the previous Sunday, only fifteen people had attended his service, compared to the one thousand who attended Elder Woodruff's meetings. Other nearby ministers were also upset and decided they were not going to watch their membership rolls decline without a fight.

The first hint of trouble came one night just as Elder Woodruff stood to begin speaking. A uniformed man entered the building, announcing that he had been sent by the rector of the parish and had a warrant to arrest the Mormon missionary.

"For what crime?" Elder Woodruff asked.

"For preaching to the people."

"I told him that I had a license for preaching the gospel to the people and that if he would take a chair, I would wait upon him after the meeting." For an hour and fifteen minutes, the officer listened to a powerful sermon on the first principles of the gospel. The speech was accompanied by an outpouring of the Spirit of God that touched many hearts. Afterwards, the constable arose slowly, emotion showing on his face.

"Mr. Woodruff," he said solemnly, "I would like to be baptized."[4]

Wilford was delighted to oblige. Besides the constable, there were seven other people who were baptized that night.

The constable returned to the rector and informed the disappointed man that if he wanted Elder Woodruff arrested for preaching, he would have to go himself and serve the writ. He then testified that he had heard Elder Woodruff preach the only true gospel sermon he had ever listened to in his life.

Frustrated, the rector decided to try again. This time, he sent two clerks of the Church of England to spy on the meetings and find out what doctrines were being taught. Again the Spirit of the Lord filled those present, including the two would-be spies, who afterwards asked to be baptized. After these failures, the rector dared not send any more people to Elder Woodruff's meetings.

However, other ministers and rectors continued to try to rid themselves of the successful missionary. They held a convention and drafted a petition, which they sent to the Archbishop of Canterbury. In it, they asked Parliament to pass a law prohibiting the Mormons from preaching in Britain. The Archbishop and his council replied that the law of England denied no religion the right to preach. To the peevish ministers, he declared that "if they had the worth of souls at heart as much as they had the ground where hares, foxes and hounds ran, they would not lose so many of their flock."[5]

Despite all attempts to thwart him, Brother Woodruff continued to preach and baptize. On March 21st, he baptized Thomas Kingston, the Superintendent of the Preachers and Members of the United Brethren. After just thirty days in Herefordshire, Elder Woodruff had baptized forty-five preachers and 160 members of the United Brethren. This group then gave him access to a chapel and forty-five houses that were licensed for preaching.

"This opened a wide field for labor and enabled me to bring into the Church, through the blessing of God, over 1,800 souls during eight months," stated Elder Woodruff, "including all of the 600 United Brethren except one person. In this number there were also two hundred preachers of various denominations. The power of God rested upon us and upon the mission. The whole history of this Herefordshire mission shows the importance of listening to the still small voice of the Spirit of God and the revelations of the Holy Ghost."[6]

Notes

1. Matthias F. Cowley, *Wilford Woodruff*, (Salt Lake City: Deseret News, 1909), p. 116.

2. Ibid., pp. 116–117.

3. Ibid., p. 117.

4. Ibid., p. 118.

5. Ibid., p. 119.

6. Ibid., pp. 119–120.

Chapter 12

John M. Bohn

ESCAPE BEHIND A FODDER BOX

A particularly vivid nightmare caused Elder John M. Bohn to have a sleepless night in December of 1852. In his dream, he was crossing an open field when a great carnivorous monster began chasing him. Terrified, Elder Bohn searched frantically for a way to escape the beast. Seeing a thick cluster of trees and brush, he raced to it, knowing that he would be safe from the ghastly monster if only he could get past this thicket. However, as he was clawing his way through, he became entangled in the brush. It took all the strength he could muster to tear loose from the brambles and vines that wrapped themselves around him like the tentacles of a deadly octopus. Finally, after much struggling, John was able to free himself and escape from the beast.

Elder Bohn was worried and confused about what this

strange and terrifying dream could mean. As he discussed it with his companion, Elder Poulsen, the Spirit blessed him with understanding and he told his companion that the dream meant that snares would be laid for him by sectarian priestcraft. The great carnivorous beast represented Satan, who desired to have him and all who spread the word of God. Although enemies of the Church would try to entangle him, in the end, the Lord would deliver him unharmed.

It was a cold and snowy winter on the island of Lolland, Denmark. Elder Bohn had never been in the best of health and was frequently ill. Although some of the people on Lolland were hostile toward Mormons, the missionaries were happy to teach the gospel to those few who were interested in their message. Elder Bohn said wryly that actually teaching lessons made a nice change from receiving threats.

On the morning after the dream, the missionaries went to the village of Thoreby, which lay on the east end of Lolland. Only thirteen members of the Church lived on the island and the elders hoped to increase that number. They were pleased when several of their meetings were well attended. That Saturday night, they baptized eleven people.

On Sunday, Elder Swenson, who presided over the mission, asked Elder Poulsen to accompany him to another area. He thought it would be best for Elder Bohn, who had recently been quite ill, not to travel. Elder Bohn's latest illness, when he had been coughing up blood, had been caused by traveling for miles in the freezing snow with wet feet. Since the missionary had not yet fully recovered, Elder Swenson asked him to stay behind and conduct a fast meeting.

When it came time for the meeting, Elder Bohn walked to the nearby home of Niels Jensen, where the members were rejoicing over having eleven converts join them. As the meeting progressed, the missionary stood to officiate at the sacrament table but stopped when the door opened. In walked a minister from a local Church, followed by his deacon and a large group of people. The minister proudly strutted into the room, apparently hoping to disturb the Saints, as some of them were former members of his congregation. The room was soon completely filled, as was the small hall. Those who couldn't crowd in stood outside. Thinking it would be best to ignore the disrupters, Elder Bohn bowed his head and said the sacrament prayer.

Although the atmosphere was tense, it remained quiet during the sacrament service. Then, in a raspy voice, Elder Bohn spoke on the sufferings of Christ and about the Atonement He had made for a fallen world. The elder's voice cracked a few times as he reminded the members of the covenants they had made with God at baptism and of their duty toward God and toward each other.

The missionary's voice grew fainter and fainter until finally it disappeared altogether. When he stopped, Elder Bohn felt so weak and ill that he thought he would have to end the meeting early. However, as the audience watched and waited, Elder Bohn closed his eyes and whispered a prayer. After a few minutes, he began to speak again. His voice became clear and strong and he continued his talk for a full hour, discussing the various aspects of the plan of salvation.

Elder Bohn said that he stated the plan so clearly and

understandably, that he "left the priest and his people no excuse for failing to accept the only way to escape the judgments of God by becoming members of the true Church of God."[1] Finally, the Spirit told him to stop speaking.

When all was quiet, the minister, accompanied by four or five men, strode to the front of the room and smiled broadly at the congregation. "My own dear church people," he began entreatingly, "I must admit that I have listened to the honorable gentleman's speech with great interest. But when he tells us that the missionaries are the true messengers of God, sent to invite all mankind to be reconciled to Him, to escape the coming wrath, I must indeed protest, for you all know that Thoreby congregation is very good and God-like."

The men who stood beside him were each holding a large brandy bottle from which they had been drinking freely. At the minister's complimentary words, they began pounding the floor with their heavy oak sticks, swearing and hollering their agreement.

Elder Bohn glanced at them, then at the priest, before commenting dryly, "Now, your own church folks have sealed your testimony of your congregation's godliness."

"There is some scabby sheep in every flock," the minister muttered in embarrassment. The minister and the missionary then engaged in a lengthy debate. At one point, the minister turned to the audience and, waving his arm in an expansive gesture, spoke to those who had left his congregation.

"My former church members, I feel very sorry for you, especially for the young folks, at being led astray from Jesus by those vagrant Mormons; for when you die you cannot have a

Christian burial, but must be cast outside and be put in the potters field among murderers and suicides."

"Listen my friends," Elder Bohn jumped in. "It will not profit a man if he gains all worldly honor and riches if he loses his soul. . . . But those who are reckoned as the outcasts of the world, yet have walked in the straight and narrow way to the end of their mortal lives, will be raised out of their graves to meet their Redeemer in the clouds of heaven and reign under Him as kings and priests to God and the Lamb forevermore." There was silence for many moments. Then the people began to whisper among themselves.

"The Mormon priest is right," one man declared, summarizing the feelings of the majority of the people. Frustrated, the minister made a move as if to leave, then stopped and spoke loudly: "I will go now, for I see I cannot persuade that gentleman to be a Christian and he cannot make a Mormon of me."

This seemed to be a cue for the drunken men to push forward. "All right," they shouted, "We will baptize that Mormon priest in his own blood!"[2]

Someone threw a rock that knocked over and extinguished the candle on the table. Elder Bohn asked for another but was soon surrounded in the darkness by the rough men who struck the table and floor with their thick oak sticks while cursing the Mormons. At that moment, a chill went up Elder Bohn's spine as suddenly, his dream in all its sharp horror, vividly replayed itself in his mind. He felt impressed that the nightmare had now become a terrible reality. In a flash, he realized that the men and women now surrounding him represented the thick growth of trees that had entangled him in his dream. Elder

Bohn recalled that although getting through the thicket of his dream had taken all his strength, he had managed to escape in the end. He could only hope that this living nightmare would have a similar ending.

A friend pushed through toward him. "Mr. Bohn," he whispered urgently, "you had better get out of here or else you will be killed!"[3]

Those were his feelings exactly. Ducking and pushing, the missionary forced his way through the people in the darkness. When he reached a door, he yanked it open and found himself in a small room. He tried to open the tiny window but it was locked. Yanking and tugging, Elder Bohn forced it open and squeezed through.

The full moon made it much lighter outside the house than inside. He could see that many of the mob were in the yard, cutting off his escape route. There was, however, a box near the house where the Jensens kept fodder for the cattle. Letting himself down the wall, Elder Bohn crept behind the box and covered himself with the rye bundles.

Excited shouts of the raging mob split the frosty air. "Where is the Mormon?"

"Where is he?"

One woman called out, "He went into the bedroom!"[4] The mob went on a rampage, tearing the house apart as they searched for the missionary. They even destroyed the featherbed the Jensens had made to take with them to America when they emigrated.

It was a bitterly cold night. As Elder Bohn shivered under

the dusty bundles, his teeth began chattering. He was anxious about his daybook, which he had accidentally left inside the house on the windowsill as he squirmed through the narrow window. There were sixty Latter-day Saint hymns in it that he had written. He earnestly wished the book was safe with him as he listened to the dreadful shouts and racket as the mob tore down the stones of the well. A short time later, the missionary heard a wagon pull into the yard. A deep voice called out, "What is going on here? Is it murder or robbery?"[5] The mob melted into the shadows.

When all was quiet, Elder Bohn stood up, scattering the rye sheafs. Shocked, he saw that the mob in its fury had torn a number of bricks off the house. Sadly, he poked about in the rubble, searching. Suddenly, he stopped and smiled. There, lying unharmed on top of a small pile of mortar and brick, was his daybook, whole and unharmed. In later years, those hymns, together with thirteen others, would be translated into Swedish and sung for more than forty years in Scandinavian meetings.

Elder Bohn heard someone exclaim, "Oh, Brother Bohn, are you alive? We thought you dead!" He turned to see Sister Jensen, whose temple was bleeding and swollen.

"The Lord has sheltered me from all harm," he replied thankfully.[6] Indeed, he was better off than they were. A twelve-year-old boy standing near Sister Jensen had a bruised and sore chest. His ribs had nearly been broken when he was hit by flying bricks. After consoling them, Elder Bohn asked for his jacket, cap, and cane. His jacket was in one piece but his cane was gone and his cap had been torn to bits.

"I felt glad that my head was not in it when the mob tore it," Elder Bohn said wryly.[7] Afraid that the mob might return or go to his previous lodgings, he was forced to trudge seven miles through the snow on a bitterly cold night to reach a safe shelter. Though Elder Bohn was faint, chilled and hungry, the moon lit his path and he was strengthened by the Lord so that he could endure his journey. When the missionary reached the home of kindly Saints who took him in, they praised God for his deliverance.

Years later, Elder Bohn spoke of his gratitude at being protected during his harrowing experience. "Now after more than forty-three years, I can clearly see that my Heavenly Father at many times protected my body, which was never very strong and robust, from harm. . . . From the depths of my heart I feel to exclaim, 'All thanks, praise, honor and glory be to God and the Lamb forever!'"[8]

Notes

1. "Early Missionary Experience," *Juvenile Instructor, Vol. 31*, 1896, p. 206.

2. Ibid., pp. 206–207.

3. Ibid., p. 107.

4. Ibid.

5. Ibid., p. 208.

6. Ibid.

7. Ibid.

8. Ibid.

Chapter 13

Samuel W. Jenkinson

"I Always Act On My Impressions"

Even though Samuel W. Jenkinson had been studying for two years at a theological seminary to become a minister, he couldn't help but stop on the street and listen in wonder at the doctrine two missionaries from The Church of Jesus Christ of Latter-day Saint were preaching. He had come home to Lowell, Massachusetts, for a brief vacation and had been walking along a road when he paused to listen to the elders.

Samuel had been born in 1850 to a deeply religious woman who had named him after a biblical prophet. His mother had dedicated her son at birth to become a minister of the gospel, although at that time, there was no particular church she wanted him to join. When Samuel was twenty-five, he had entered the seminary to begin training for the ministry.

And now suddenly, he found himself intrigued with another church's message. Still, Samuel had always been one to act upon any impression he received, and so he invited the missionaries to his home. As they explained their beliefs more fully, Samuel found their precepts to his liking. After a thorough investigation and much prayer, he developed a testimony and was baptized a member of the Church.

Three months after his conversion, Samuel traveled to Utah where he married and eventually had three children. During the next few years, he learned the business of upholstering furniture. It was difficult work at times, as his eyesight had been very poor since he was thirteen. At that young age, Samuel had come down with scarlet fever. The illness had severely damaged his eyes, although he could still see. Samuel was an intellectual man and, even though it put a strain on his weakened eyes, he liked to read and study in the evenings.

Samuel was working at the furniture store one day when everything suddenly went dark. The doctor told him that the optic nerves of both eyes had given out. Thus, at age thirty-six, Samuel was left blind. Hoping for a miracle, he went to many doctors, but each one told him there was no hope of regaining his eyesight.

To make up for his lack of sight, Samuel decided to improve his mind. After asking his wife if she would read and write for him, he began studying theology, science, art and astronomy. With Samuel's analytical mind and remarkable memory, he soon excelled in his studies and became a member of a scientific society. He became so knowledgeable that he began giving lectures on philosophy and science.

Although he was now sightless, Brother Jenkinson continued to be active in the Church and was called to be in the superintendency of the Sunday School. Later, he became superintendent of the Mutual Improvement Association. Samuel also served as a block teacher (home teacher) for over twenty years. A skilled orator, he was constantly in demand as a speaker and lecturer and was frequently asked to speak at funerals. At the time of his death, he had spoken at over six thousand services.

After losing his sight, Brother Jenkinson and his wife had seven more children. Although his speaking fees didn't always cover their needs, he remained patient and faithful, trusting that Heavenly Father would help provide for his family.

In the late 1800's, services for the blind were woefully inadequate. Samuel thought there had to be some way to assist the blind to become self-supporting. He felt strongly that blind people could be trained to lead more socially satisfying and economically productive lives than they were now living.

As he became acquainted with other blind adults in the area, Samuel believed that many of them would benefit from training. He began to dream of a workshop, a center, that would allow the blind to socialize with each other while learning how to be independent and self-supporting. However, in order to acquire a building and launch and maintain such a program, it would be necessary for the state to render financial aid. Samuel knew that in order to convince the government of the need for such a center, he would have to enlist public support and do solid research to back up his convictions.

Launching such a massive project was not easy for someone who was blind, but Samuel acted upon his impression that this proposal was something that needed doing and that he was the man for the job. He spent the entire year of 1908 traveling throughout Utah, contacting the blind, asking questions about their health and living conditions and learning more about their attitudes and feelings. The great majority expressed a desire to work, and the results of his research made him more convinced than ever that Utah needed a workshop for the blind.

Samuel met with local government officials and presented his findings, laying out before them, not only the problems the blind faced, but solutions to those problems. He told the officials that Utah needed a workshop where the blind could meet together and receive training on how to earn a living.

While he waited for their decision, Samuel continued to travel, making home visits to teach and assist the blind. Although he was restricted in this endeavor because of his limited financial resources, his work paved the way for the later success of another mobile teacher, Murray B. Allen, who was aided by the state and became a traveling teacher for the blind.

Brother Jenkinson managed to secure two free railway passes to California to visit a workshop that had enjoyed great success in training and employing the blind. He and his wife traveled to Oakland and learned much from this well-managed shop, which made brushes, brooms, and other cleaning implements. Excited by their achievements, Samuel returned to Utah and reported his findings to Governor William Spry.

He expounded his viewpoint that the blind could and should be helped into full social and economic citizenship and enjoy the privileges that most took for granted.

Finally, Brother Jenkinson was able to convince the governor that Utah needed to begin a more comprehensive program to aid the blind and was greatly influential in the decision to create legislation that would help the blind. Because of Samuel's diligence and hard work, a bill was passed by the eighth session of the Utah State Legislature on March 22nd, 1909, which created the Utah Commission for the Adult Blind. Directed by a board of five trustees, with the governor as its president, the commission's principal duties were:

1. To set up and maintain a register of blind people.
2. To establish, equip, and maintain workshops for the industrial training and employment of the adult blind.
3. To maintain a bureau of information to aid in finding employment and in developing home industries.
4. To furnish materials and tools to use in the homes of the blind or in the commission's workshops.
5. To assist the blind to market their handiwork and products.[1]

When the Utah Commission for the Adult Blind met in the Governor's office on December 13th, 1909, they discussed what types of work would be suitable for the shop and discussed chair caning, brush making, basket weaving, and piano tuning. One unique feature of this law was that it provided temporary lodging and support, which would assist the adult blind in acquiring training and/or employment. Samuel was appointed superintendent of the workshop at a salary of $65.00 a month. The Church of Jesus Christ of Latter-day Saints donated working quarters for the venture, which was located at the back of the Lion House.

Brother Jenkinson's next task was to seek out blind people who wanted to learn a trade. He advertised the workshop by distributing flyers and by placing notices in the newspapers. Within two years, the size of the monthly payroll had increased almost tenfold.

Many people were grateful for the opportunity to become self-sufficient. One such person was Else Marie Peirath. She had lost her eyesight at the age of eight, following a severe case of scarlet fever. After becoming converted to the gospel in 1899, Else had traveled to Utah where she became employed as a housekeeper. In her spare time, she knitted and crocheted. When Else learned about the workshop, she immediately applied and Samuel was delighted to take on someone who already had some training. Else did so well that she was soon made a teacher and her salary was doubled to $1.00 per day.

An older blind man, James Standing, came to Samuel at the age of sixty. "He sharpened the knives for cutting the reed used in cane seats for chairs and operated the trimming machine which trimmed and evened bristles of the different kinds of brushes. Each member of his family was given a clothes brush made by their father."[2]

Samuel was kept busy, since most of the management for the workshop fell on his shoulders. In fact, the shop was so dependent upon him, that it was forced to close when he died suddenly in 1911.

Besides his occupational work for the blind, Brother Jenkinson felt strongly about performing saving ordinances for the dead and labored extensively in the temple. An interesting story associated with doing temple work began on a Sunday when a man, simply referred to as Brother P, decided on the spur of the moment to attend the sacrament services at the 20th Ward. It so happened that Brother Jenkinson was speaking there that day. Brother P was so impressed with his remarks that he wrote to the blind man, complimenting him on his talk.

Some time later, Samuel called Brother P and said, "Your telephone number has been coming to me for a week, especially while I was in the temple. . . . Today the number 5279 came to me so many times that, on leaving the temple, I have come to phone. Now I do not know what to say to you."[3]

The two men agreed to meet and talk. During their conversation, Brother P mentioned that his wife had recently died. Six weeks later, Samuel telephoned Brother P with some startling news.

"I am impressed that your wife wants her temple work done," Brother Jenkinson announced.[4] Brother P said he would see to it and went to the presiding officer of the temple to discuss the matter. The usual procedure was to wait until one year after the date of death before having the ordinance work done. After some discussion, both men decided it would be best to wait the usual amount of time. However, some time later, President Winder felt impressed that he should make an exception in Sister P's case. He then went to the authorities to request permission to do the work earlier than was customary. When Samuel rang Brother P later to find out how the work had gone, he was surprised to discover it had been put off. He gave the man a short and vigorous sermon.

"You have let ten days go by and haven't done that work for your wife yet. I am impressed with the feeling that your wife wants her temple work done, and I always act on my impressions." The blind temple worker went on, "If her temple work is done, she will have more happiness and greater freedom, can progress faster and further and can accomplish much more for herself and for others and for you right here on earth." He then paused, deciding that Brother P should be allowed to make his own decision. "But you can do what you want. I hereby clear myself from all responsibility and leave it wholly to you."

Brother P remembered how his wife had always told him not to procrastinate, saying, "Tomorrow has enough duties of its own to attend to, so don't crowd the duties of today on tomorrow." Feeling repentant, he replied contritely, "I am convinced, Brother Jenkinson, and will see to it at once."[5]

Taking the next train to Ogden, Brother P went to see his sister and asked her to stand in as proxy for his wife. His sister was astonished to see him at her door, as she was just about to write him because of an astonishing dream she'd had. She had dreamed about his wife and felt it was her wish to have her temple work done. The temple work was done promptly, partly because a courageous man felt prompted to act upon his impressions.

Notes

1. Phillip Reed Clinger, "*History of the Utah Commission for the Adult Blind, 1909–1956.*"

2. Kate B. Carter, *Heart Throbs of the West, Vol. 10*, (Salt Lake City: Daughters of Utah Pioneers), p. 352.

3. George C. Lambert, *Treasures In Heaven, Fifteenth Book of the Faith Promoting Series*, (Juvenile Instructor Office), p. 59.

4. Ibid.

5. Ibid., pp. 60–61.

Chapter 14

Niels P. L. Eskildz

A HARD CROSS TO BEAR

It was a simple job he'd done many times, but this time, ten-year-old Niels felt a strange foreboding about bringing the cow in from pasture. However, his parents insisted, so he went, carrying a rope that he would use to lead the animal. On the way home, the cow became frightened and plunged about wildly, tangling Niels up in the rope. The frightened cow dragged the young boy through the fields, hurling him against obstructions. His injuries were so serious that Niels was bedfast more than five years. To pass the time while he was in bed, his mother read to her youngest child and taught him needlework.

Niels P. L. Eskildz was born May 31, 1836, in Denmark. Although his three older siblings were large, brawny men, Niels was short and bent because of the accident. His spine was so curved and deformed that it looked like his body had been crumpled over by some mighty force that had thrust his head down between his shoulders. After many years spent in bed, Niels was able to get up and hobble around on crutches.

In 1850, the apostle Erastus Snow arrived in Denmark to preach the gospel. Although fourteen-year-old Niels didn't attend any meetings, he learned a little about Mormonism from his minister who went to some of the meetings. Although the minister became acquainted with the doctrine and seemed to believe it, he couldn't bring himself to be baptized.

When it came time for Niels to be confirmed a member of the Lutheran Church, the priest said: "The Lord has laid a heavy hand upon you in your youth, which will be a hard cross for you to bear through life; but it was for a wise purpose, to prepare you for a great work that you do not understand now. After you have traveled thousands of miles to a strange land you know not, you will there eventually have a chance to go into the sanctuary of the Lord to do a work for your father's family and your ancestors that they did not understand or know anything about."[1]

Such an unusual prediction made a deep impression on Niels, although he thought it quite improbable that a confirmed invalid with no money should ever travel thousands of miles. As for going to the sanctuary of the Lord and performing a work for his ancestors, Niels could not even begin to guess what that could mean.

During the next six years, Niels gained a small measure of strength and agility. When he turned twenty, the young man went to live with his brother but was often left with the feeling that he was in the way. By chance, a lady discovered that Niels was skilled in needlework and encouraged him to take sewing up as a trade. Happy with the fine work he did, she recommended Niels to her rich, aristocratic friends, bringing him much needed work.

Then Niels had another chance to learn more about Mormonism. As he investigated the Church, he felt the doctrine was sound. However, the religion was so unpopular and he was so dependent upon others that Neils felt he would not be able to support himself if people turned away from him if he was baptized.

His crippled, dependent condition was a great source of sorrow to Niels, especially when he saw how repelled people were by his hunched and twisted body. Because of the discord between his brother, sister-in-law and himself, Niels moved into a small, lonely apartment in Aalborg. Feeling forsaken and depressed, he began brooding upon his life. Months passed in gloom and loneliness. Just as misery was about to overpower him, Niels had an epiphany that dramatically changed his attitude.

It happened on a day when Niels was feeling especially despondent. He was just starting to fix dinner when a grand vision opened up to him. He described it as a series of scenes, which he later compared to modern moving pictures. Niels was shown his existence in the spirit world, prior to his mortal birth. After this view of the pre-mortal existence, he saw not only his mortal life on earth, but what future reward he would be worthy of in the next life. Niels understood that he had seen this panorama of his mortal life and the life hereafter once before—in the pre-mortal existence. The handicapped man was allowed to remember that before his birth, he had been given the opportunity of choosing the class of reward he wanted to gain when his mortal life was over.

Niels recalled that he had deliberately made a choice as to what trials he would suffer on earth. He also remembered specifically which rewards he had chosen to try for, understanding that the glorious rewards he had chosen could only be gained by persevering through great mortal suffering. Niels was conscious of the fact that he had insisted upon a certain reward and had understood, accepted, and agreed to all the conditions he would have to face after coming to earth. During this spiritual manifestation, the young man's understanding of his own life was heightened and magnified. When the vision faded, Niels realized that to rebel against his present fate was a base violation of the promise and agreement he had entered into long ago in the pre-mortal existence and was a reproach to his divine Father.

Niels realized that others might ridicule the vision but knew without a doubt that it came from God and was an answer to his prayers. This manifestation helped him form a new philosophy of life and he developed an unshakable faith in God and gained a new, clear knowledge of the purpose of mortal life. For the rest of his life, Niels derived comfort and fortitude from this profound revelation. As a result, he was determined to be stalwart and uncomplaining and to do the best he could in spite of his many handicaps and afflictions.

Although he didn't become a lighthearted or jovial person, Niels developed a new serenity and thereafter refused to complain about his disability. He felt the Lord had granted him the vision for a wise and merciful purpose and considered it a tremendous blessing. Niels knew the manifestation was given to enable him to have a better understanding of his duty and to strengthen him so that he could remain steadfast and true in spite of his trials.

With new confidence in God and in himself, Niels began investigating The Church of Jesus Christ of Latter-day Saints more fully. Then, the young man found that the Lord was continuing to work on his behalf. One stormy night, a missionary, Elder Kempe, knocked at his door. Elder Kempe said that an angel had awakened him in the night and told to get up and go baptize Brother Eskildz. Not one to argue with an angel, Niels was baptized on November 1, 1862.

Like other Saints in Scandinavia, Niels had a strong desire to migrate to Zion but he was stuck with the almost insurmountable problem of how to obtain money for his fare. It seemed to be a problem with no solution, as his income came mainly from charity and his own earnings were very meager. Then one day, a priest told him that a benefactor had died, leaving a legacy that was to be given to someone who was physically helpless and dependent. After making an application to the parish, Brother Eskildz was granted the legacy, which amounted to forty dollars a year. He began saving the greater part of it for his emigration.

However, trouble arose when leaders in the parish learned that he had been baptized into The Church of Jesus Christ. The quarterly payments of ten dollars were immediately cut off. Offended, Niels went to the parish. He told them they had no right to apply any religious test to him, as the benefactor had not stipulated that the money was to be used only for people of their faith. After some discussion, they said Niels could have the legacy for a limited time. The handicapped man refused this concession, telling them that because of his poor health, he was not liable to live very long. However, he offered to make a settlement. If they would advance him twelve quarterly payments, amounting to $120.00, he would surrender his right to any more. They agreed and Niels began making preparations to migrate to Utah.

Brother Eskildz was almost ready to leave when his asthma—something he had suffered from for many years—flared up. He became seriously ill. At times, Niels had so much difficulty breathing that he was not able to lie down but had to sleep while sitting up. His condition worsened and, because of his frail and weakened state, his acquaintances feared that if he continued with his plans, he would die while trying to cross the ocean. Yet Niels would not abandon his immigration plans. Determined to join the Saints, he paid a newly married couple and a young single man to look after his luggage and care for him during the journey.

In 1866, Niels left his homeland, embarking on a voyage that took eight weeks. Gradually, his health improved. After arriving in America, the group of Saints traveled to Nebraska by railroad. They were packed into a cattle car, where they were endlessly jarred and pitched about on the hard floor. For relief from the jarring, Brother Eskildz braced his hands against the floor on either side of him, but it did little good. The jolting was so extreme that both doors fell off the boxcar before they reached their destination.

After arriving in Nebraska, Niels made final preparations to travel by ox train to Salt Lake City. All able-bodied passengers were requested to walk as much as possible to conserve the strength of the heavily-loaded oxen. Although Brother Eskildz had not been able to walk even two hundred yards before leaving Denmark without stopping to rest, he tried to do his part. Yet, even at his best, he could not keep up with the ox train. Niels tried to compensate for his snail's pace by starting out early in the morning, leaving hours before the others began. He would walk until the main group overtook him or until he was so exhausted that he could go no further. Then and only then, would he give in and ride.

Occasionally, there were days when, by virtue of his strong will and persistent nature, he succeeded in walking all day. But this could only be accomplished if Niels started out hours before the camp arose in the morning and continued for hours after the camp had stopped for the night. On several occasions, while trying to find his way in the dark, he became lost. But by praying, he was able to find which way the Saints had gone. Eventually he would catch up, although with his crutches and the uneven trail, it was hard to hobble along quickly in the darkness.

During the journey, Niels was blessed to be cured of the asthma that had afflicted him for so long. He was also blessed with uncommon strength, so that despite his severe handicap, he was able to walk more than three-fourths of the way across the plains.

The man from Denmark possessed great will power and a strong and independent mind for one whose body was so fragile. Brother Eskildz was always sedate, reserved, and self-possessed. His deep respect for the rights and feelings of others was no doubt developed by his having been so helplessly dependent upon others the greater part of his life. Although the difficulty of such a long, arduous journey sometimes caused disputes among members of the group, Niels remained on good terms with all. During the trip, he gained a reputation as a peacemaker and was frequently asked to be an arbitrator and achieve a reconciliation between arguing parties. A keen observer, Brother Eskildz was a good listener and had a logical and discriminating mind.

Occasionally he was heard to say, "The tongue is a dangerous member if allowed to wag too freely."[2]

Upon his arrival in the Salt Lake Valley, Niels immediately sought work. His first job, located only through great and persistent effort, was to make buckskin gloves. It had been difficult to persuade his employers to hire a disabled man and they did so only after Niels said they would not have to pay him while he learned the business. He only asked that once he became skilled, they would furnish him with work when they had more than they could do. It was a precarious job and not well paid, but Brother Eskildz did not want to be dependent upon others. When demand for the gloves fell, he began sewing uppers for ladies shoes. But soon, machines displaced his hand sewing.

Thereafter, Niels sought work at whatever he could manage but sometimes ill health kept him at home. On those occasions, he had to live on his meager savings until he could get well enough to work again. Brother Eskildz lived a life of poverty. Sometimes he suffered from lack of food because he was once turned away by uncharitable people after asking for help and he was determined to go without rather than face such humiliation again.

Many times, however, Niels was blessed by an unseen hand. At night, he might scrape up the last saucerful of flour in his larder to make a small cake, only to discover the next morning that there was flour still remaining in the sack.

As the years passed, Brother Eskildz managed to save five dollars, which he put down on a lot, although he was hard pressed every year to pay the small amount of taxes due on it. Then came the real estate boom of 1888 and he was able to sell the property for $500. Never had Niels imagined that one day he would own his own home, but after selling his lot, his dream came true when he was able to buy a small house.

Brother Eskildz had never forgotten the blessing given him as a boy at the hands of the priest and in his later years, became anxious to do something for his ancestors who had died without a knowledge of the Church. When the temple in Logan was completed, Niels wanted to share the blessings of the gospel with his ancestors and so made the journey to Cache Valley, where he spent eight weeks doing ordinance work for his dead relatives. There was something exalting to Niels about the thought that he, a sickly, deformed person, could do something for the salvation of his kindred dead and departed friends that no one else in the world could do.

One day, Niels was surprised to receive a letter from an old acquaintance, Brother Nielsen, who asked if he would come to visit. He went to see his friend who was very ill and expected to die soon. Brother Nielsen explained that he had hoped to do the temple work for his relatives when the Manti temple was finished but after its dedication, he had became very ill. He had moved north to Salt Lake City to live with his daughter, hoping to recover, but instead his condition had worsened. Brother Nielsen worried constantly over the fact that the temple work that he had set his heart upon had not been done. Feeling death was not far away, the ill man had remembered Niels and felt prompted to contact him. He begged Niels to do the work in the temple that he was now unable to finish.

Brother Eskildz agreed to help and wrote down the names of seventy of his friend's relatives. Feeling at peace after receiving assurance that the work would be done, Brother Nielsen passed away. Niels traveled to Manti to fulfill his friend's request. He had been told that Brother Nielsen's sister would do the work for the females but when he arrived, found that she was very ill herself. He then located other women to do the work and spent ten weeks of constant, joyful labor in the Manti temple.

Happy and content, Niels felt like he had found his true vocation and decided to devote all the time to the temple that his health and means would permit. He was overjoyed when the Salt Lake Temple was dedicated and he could begin working there.

Still expert at sewing, Niels found work stitching temple clothing. Although he was not able to work continuously—as he was frequently ill—he became known as one of the most earnest and devoted workers in the temple. After completing the temple work for his own ancestors, Niels found others who wanted to have their ancestors' work done and assisted them in completing their ordinance work.

It was very difficult for Niels to walk from his home to the temple—a distance of about one mile. Already handicapped, he was further burdened by a worn-out body and advancing years. However, by leaning heavily upon his crutch, he was able to move slowly but steadily. He never betrayed his physical agony by word or facial expression.

When he was seventy-four, Niels lost his voice and was never again able to talk above a whisper. By that time, he had officiated for at least 2,200 people, besides sponsoring the work for many females. Niels remained true and faithful in the gospel despite his many hardships and frequently declared that he was deeply indebted to the gospel for all the comfort he ever had. His forbearance under such severe physical handicaps show him to be a man of tremendous courage and faith.

Notes

1. George C. Lambert, *Treasures In Heaven, Fifteenth Book of the Faith Promoting Series,* (Salt Lake City: Juvenile Instructor Office, 1914), p. 12.

2. Ibid., p. 14.

Chapter 15

Louise Lake

A MIRACLE IN MODERN ISRAEL

As president of the Young Women's Mutual Improvement Association, thirty-year-old Louise Lake felt it would be a wonderful experience for the youth in her area to visit Carthage Jail. They made their plans and in the fall of 1945, visited that historic site. However, while the group was there, a strange but growing fatigue almost kept Louise from bearing her testimony until a powerful Spirit prompted her to get up. Afterwards, she was glad she did, for it was the last time she would be able to stand on her feet without aid.

The next morning when Louise tried to walk, her legs seemed to fold beneath her. They had become numb by the time an ambulance, with flashing lights and a wailing siren, had raced her to the hospital in St. Louis. They discovered that Louise had been stricken with polio. An iron lung was brought in to help the young mother breathe, even though the doctors felt there was no hope. Louise prayed to be allowed to live to raise Jane, her little girl, but her condition became critical when one of her lungs collapsed. Then, she lapsed into a coma.

When Sister Lake finally woke, her hands and arms were paralyzed and she was burning with fever. She was extremely thirsty and managed with a great effort to turn her head. Although there was a pitcher full of water and a glass on the table beside her, the stricken woman had no power to reach out. When Louise realized she was unable to even press the call button, she panicked and cried out for help. A nurse in a starched white uniform opened the screened-off area and came over, a white gauze mask covering her dark face.

Feeling frightened, alone and desperately in need of God's help, Louise asked the nurse to pray with her. The compassionate nurse went to the door and closed it against prying eyes. Then, knowing she was risking her career, the nurse dropped the isolation mask and took off her gloves. Taking the risk of contagion, she took Louise's two helpless hands.

Lowering her head, the nurse murmured, "You'll have to pray, I can't." In a short but sincere and faithful prayer, Louise sought for strength to endure. Then she thanked Heavenly Father for the relief that had come in the form of the angel nurse. When she looked up, tears were flooding down the attendant's face.

"I would give anything and have no fears if I knew God like that and could pray to him that way," the nurse said.[1]

The next day, Louise's oldest sister, Sarah, was holding a

vigil outside her hospital room when a doctor stopped and gently told her that Louise would not last long. Shortly afterwards, the branch president and three other men arrived and asked if they could give the ill woman a blessing. The doctors refused, saying it was too late to pray for a woman that was more dead than alive. The brethren insisted and were finally allowed to enter. Miraculously, Sister Lake woke as they began praying, feeling as though she were fighting her way through a dense fog. Unable to speak, she nevertheless heard them blessing her to live.

Gradually, Louise began to improve. A week later, the president of the local mission and Elder Joseph F. Merrill, an Apostle, visited her. Elder Merrill told the ill woman that she was standing on the threshold of eternity and that if she lived, it would be due to her faith.

Miraculously, Louise did live. During the next three weeks, she recovered enough that she could be sent to a hospital in Salt Lake City. Unfortunately, for three long months, little was done to help her. Then, Louise was sent to LDS Hospital. They placed a bar across the bed to allow her to try to develop more strength in her arms but provided no other method of therapy. Realizing that her rehabilitation was in her own hands, Louise planned out and began a series of vigorous exercises.

There were many visitors who helped the ill woman pass the time. One of her favorites was her little girl Jane, who was being cared for by relatives who lived nearby. Once, Elder Joseph F. Merrill strode into her room unannounced. During their conversation, Louse expressed her desire to get better so she could do missionary work.

"You *are* on a mission," he declared soberly.[2]

One day, when a pretty nurse mentioned that she needed a hat for her upcoming wedding, Louise asked if she could make it. Soon, her hospital bed was covered with needles, thread, and trimmings. The venture turned out to be good therapy, because the struggle to make the stitches neat and strong strengthened the patient's hands. The hat was such a great success that Louise ended up making fifteen hats for other nurses during her stay.

After her release from the hospital, Louise went to live with a relative. Although her sister offered to pay for a nurse to bathe her, Louise was determined to learn how to maneuver her helpless body by herself. To that end, she had her nephew build a chair that would enable her to get out of bed and go to the bathroom on her own. The first time Sister Lake tried it, she fell, and it took all of her strength and ingenuity—along with a good three hours—to inch her way along the floor to the bed, dragging the chair alongside her. When she finally made it, she was elated.

She concluded, "Cheerfulness is a product of will and of faith; it need have no limits."[3]

Louise began setting goals. Then, she planned how to accomplish them. After that, she visualized herself reaching her goals. The final step was physically following through. Through all of these steps, the determined woman asked the Lord for help.

"He was constantly there," she testified of the Lord's hand

in her life, "assisting me with ideas for better techniques, more courage, more faith. Occasionally I had blessings and prayers from the priesthood. They brought much needed comfort and at the same time pointed the way." She added thoughtfully, "You may walk through sorrow in joy if your path is lighted by faith."[4]

One particular blessing by Lynn McKinley gave her much comfort. He told her that she would bless the lives of thousands not in spite of her affliction but because of her affliction. He told Sister Lake that her voice would be raised to Heavenly Father's children in foreign lands and that, as she traveled about alone she would be known as a miracle in modern Israel.

After six months, Louise made plans to return to St. Louis, where her husband was still stationed. She was undaunted, even though she had to fly alone. The reunion didn't work out, so Louise returned to Salt Lake City. She rented a four-room apartment and friends helped make the necessary modifications to accommodate her wheelchair. Louise continued to regain the use of her muscles by cooking. She considered beating batter good therapy for strengthening weak arm muscles and disposed of the baked goods by sharing them with neighbors and by serving them at parties.

When Elder Matthew Cowley and his family moved in just two floors above her, the two became great pals. Speaking of their friendship, Louise commented good-naturedly, "In my life there have been a great many weeds, but frequently some of them burst into bloom."[5]

Four years after polio took the use of her legs, Louise received a telegram stating that her husband was ending their marriage. It took time for Louise to find a job but she was grateful when she finally did. Although her income was slight, the hard-working mother managed to support herself and her daughter. She joked that money could never burn a hole in her pocket, as it was never there long enough to get very warm.

When Louise was called to serve as president of the Young Women in her ward, she was astounded. The bishop told Sister Lake that he had also been surprised when her name came to his mind. He confided that at first, he had opposed it because of her condition, but the Lord soon convinced him otherwise.

Louise became very busy, meeting with the young people Saturday afternoons and going with them to the canyons. There in the twilight, they would play games, build campfires, have talent shows, put on plays or simply sing. A valiant leader, she attended every function, her sturdy wheelchair taking her over many rough trails. Often Louise was the chef, cooking in the picnic areas as the others played. Sometimes she would borrow enormous kettles and cook chili or beef barbecue at home, then transport it up to the mountains.

Another one of her responsibilities was supervising the young people at dances. Fortunately, there were plenty of chivalrous young men at Whitney Hall who were willing to carry her up and down the steps. Because of Sister Lake's sincere love and concern, many young men and women came to tell her of their problems and receive wise guidance. Often, she told them to be like the tea kettle: "You can be up to your neck in hot water and even let off a little steam, but the important thing is that you can sing."[6]

Brother Cowley noticed the great number of people coming to his friend's door. He once told her with a twinkle in his eye that she ought to hang out her shingle as she had more business than he did!

In March of 1958, Louise and other officers of the Young Women were invited to a special awards banquet. She wondered who the speaker, Marba C. Josephson, associate managing editor of the Improvement Era, was talking about in such glowing terms, since no name was mentioned. Finally, Marba announced she was bestowing the distinguished Honorary Golden Gleaner Award upon Louise.

As Christmas approached, Louise felt guilty because she had missed paying a full tithing for a few months. She decided her gift for the Savior on His birthday would be that of being a full tithe payer. After praying for forgiveness, the financially-strapped woman asked the Lord to inspire her to know where to borrow the ninety dollars she owed. Three days later, the postman rang the doorbell. He handed her a registered letter. Inside the Christmas card was a crisp, new hundred-dollar bill. Sister Lake immediately took it to the bishop. When he handed her back ten dollars in change, she insisted he keep it as tithing on her hundred-dollar gift.

After her daughter Jane was married, Louise quit her job and traveled to New York's Institute of Physical Medicine and Rehabilitation to have surgery that would enable her to lock her legs, thus allowing her to stand with support. She remained there for rehabilitation for a long time and got to know Dr. Howard A. Rusk, director of the institute. He was so impressed with Louise that he asked her to stay in New York and receive training to become a rehabilitation specialist. Dr. Rusk told the astonished woman that she had great potential to assist the handicapped and that he wanted her to go out and preach the gospel of rehabilitation.

Startled at first, Louise accepted and moved in with friends at the nearby mission home. After completing her training, Louise received a job offer but was still worried about her lack of degrees. Concerned, she showed the offer to Dr. Rusk. He slapped her heartily on the back and declared that her wheelchair was her degree. In 1955, she joined the staff at LDS Hospital in Salt Lake City.

After returning to Utah, Louise's life took an unexpected turn when she became involved in politics. It began when Dr. Chester A. Swinyard, the hospital's medical director, asked if she could do anything to promote House Bill 99 in the State Legislature. The bill—which was currently dying—would allow a new rehabilitation hospital to be built. Louise felt sure that if the legislators were aware of the great need for such a facility, they would support it. She decided to meet personally with each and every member of that committee in the House of Representatives.

Louise recalls, "Having had no instructions, for the first time in my life I started lobbying, as an amateur. Away I went, wheeling through the corridors under the State Capitol rotunda."[7] She had to teach cab drivers how to safely convey her up the lesser of the imposing flights of steps to the most accessible entrance. As unsuspecting representatives exited the chambers of the House, Louise would stop them and plead her case. One by one, they responded affirmatively and, in less than three weeks, House Bill 99 was brought back to life and passed.

Louise's work was not done, however. She then went to the Senate chambers on the opposite side of the building and began waylaying committee members there. Again, the bill passed. Her next trip to the Capitol resulted from a personal invitation by Governor George Dewey Clyde who extended personal congratulations on her successful efforts before signing the bill.

Her days spent at LDS Hospital were richly satisfying. Louise states:

> "During the next few months I lost myself in the exciting association with wonderful folks in wheelchairs, on gurneys and on crutches. Some individuals I worked with achieved the wonderful victory of getting in and out of bed without aid, or of standing on their feet once more even if it required the aid of braces or crutches. I saw tremendous heroism in all of those persons. How often I tried to explain to them that handicaps can be called 'detours,'" she explained. "God built the highway for us and if we stumble onto a detour . . . we will find only one successful way to deal with that detour. We must look to God, and he will lead us out again onto the highway of happiness. A detour is only a temporary by-pass."[8]

Then Louise received a telegram from Washington D.C. It brought the overwhelming news that she had been named the Outstanding Handicapped American of 1957. Bemused at having the distinguished honor to be the first woman ever to receive this award, Sister Lake traveled to the nation's capital. Shortly before the program started, a man hurried to her side, dropping the bombshell that, after the U.S. Navy Band had played, she would be asked to speak. As she stared out in glassy-eyed shock at the huge crowd, he told her to relax and enjoy the moment. Louise said a short prayer and felt a reassuring calmness. Then the President of the United States entered.

Taking her hand, President Eisenhower said, "Mrs. Lake, I know much more about you than you think I do. I have been reading the Deseret News, and a doctor wrote me a letter about you. I read it with enthusiasm. I understand you have done a wonderful work." Standing nearby was Elder Ezra Taft Benson of the Council of the Twelve who was then serving as Secretary of Agriculture.

Taking the President by the arm, Elder Benson said, "President Eisenhower, all of these lovely things you have said are true. I know this girl."

Louise rolled over to the microphone and began to speak:

> "It is a distinct honor to represent the illustrious state of Utah in receiving this plaque and it is with delight and humility and in honor that I accept it. . . . My work is not a job but a way of life. I have loved helping the handicapped individuals at the LDS Hospital in the activities of daily living. . . . Let us bring to those so-called handicapped individuals a joy in life. Let's bring them out of the attics, out of the basement rooms, into a life of productivity and joy." As she ended by saying,

> "God bless you," the great audience rose to their feet in a standing ovation.[9]

After the ceremony, Louise went to the U.S. Capitol and did a TV show with Senators Arthur V. Watkins and Wallace F. Bennett. The next day, Mrs. Eisenhower personally invited her to visit the White House and gave her an extended tour.

After returning home, Louise continued working at LDS Hospital and also found time to do volunteer work for the Utah State Polio Committee and the National Polio Foundation. Reports of her success in securing money for the Governor's Committee on Employment for the Physically Handicapped spread to Washington. President Eisenhower then appointed her to be on the President's Commission for that same cause.

In 1958, Dr. Howard A. Rusk asked her to join his staff at the Institute of Physical Medicine and Rehabilitation in New York. Sister Lake accepted and was appointed the institute's first Director of Volunteers.

The institute always received many requests for Dr. Rusk to lecture to various groups, but after Sister Lake joined his staff, he frequently turned the invitations over to Louise. She remarked wryly that Dr. Rusk was always most obliging and enthusiastic about her accepting his invitations. However, it was an honor and also the first time that a paralyzed woman, confined to a wheelchair, had traveled alone with the intent of rehabilitating others.

"It was hard work," she recalls, "but it was heart work."[10]

In 1961, Louise began working internationally on behalf

of the handicapped. She was invited by Mr. Lyman S. Shreeve, Director of the Instituto Chileno-Norte Americano de Cultura, to travel to Latin America and participate in seminars on general rehabilitation. Her two-week tour began in Vina del Mar, Chile. Sister Lake gave press conferences, visited hospitals and delivered countless lectures. Amazingly, she was able to travel from country to country alone and without knowing the language.

Louise soon realized that others looked to her as an example of what a handicapped person could attain. Amazed at her independence, officials in Latin America began to see rehabilitation as a procedure that would help people return to a normal, productive life instead of something that just wasted time, money and effort. Indeed, Sister Lake felt that her most significant contribution was cultivating positive attitudes toward the abilities of the handicapped.

While in Chile, Louise once visited a shabby rehabilitation center that had one entire section full of bed-ridden teenagers. When she asked why they were all lying down, the answer came back that because the center lacked wheelchairs, each patient could only have a one-hour stint with a wheelchair once every three days. The director explained that the reason they couldn't afford wheelchairs was because duty fees cost as much as a new wheelchair. Outraged, Louise went to work.

Ten days earlier, Sister Lake had been sitting next to Señor Luis Guevara Ortuzar, the Governor of Chile, at a banquet. She recalled that he had leaned over and told her to call upon him if he could ever assist her. Taking him at his word, she immediately called and asked for his help in waiving the custom fees on wheelchairs. Although she had to leave Chile before the matter could be settled, Louise wrote letters from Argentina and made phone calls from Buenos Aires to continue to press for changes. Because of her efforts, regulations were changed to eliminate customs fees on all rehabilitation equipment.

Even with that success, Sister Lake didn't consider her work done and began negotiating to find the best buy in wheelchairs. Working with the Catholic Relief Services, she was able to obtain a shipment of wheelchairs, which was then sent to needy rehabilitation centers in Chile.

After returning to the United States, Louise resumed work, but in January of 1962, received a cablegram from Señor Carlos LaCerda, Governor of Guanabara, Brazil. He invited her to come back to Brazil to further the work for the handicapped that she had begun during her earlier visit. When she arrived, a welcoming committee met her in Rio de Janeiro and a linguist was assigned to be her secretary. Reporters from television and newspapers kept track of Sister Lake's busy schedule.

One night, after she had given a lecture, her guests kept pressing her to drink a small silver cup of their prized "Brazilian" coffee. Louise kept saying no but eventually had to offer a tactful reason for her abstinence. Rather than drinking it, Louise politely asked if she could have a little bottle full of coffee to take with her to the beach the next day. She explained that, while her religion felt it would be harmful for her to take any coffee inwardly, she thought it would make an excellent suntan lotion. They graciously assented. Although

Louise admitted later that she had never heard of using coffee as suntan lotion, she had started a fad and many people began using it for that purpose.

Louise continued working for the handicapped. A few years later, she was invited to attend the Governor's Committee on Employment for the Physically Handicapped in Puerto Rico. She labored to assist them with programs for hiring the handicapped. At home, she was asked to help introduce a new project in the U.S. which was co-sponsored by the President's Committee on Employment for Physically Handicapped and the National Easter Seal Society. The project was called the "Architectural Barrier Project," and its aim was to remove narrow doorways and revolving doors and to provide restrooms with facilities for wheelchairs. Feeling strongly about this project, Louise took a leave of absence from work and moved to Chicago.

Speaking about the architectural project, Sister Lake declared, "Surely the Lord has no intentions for man to prohibit the disabled from entering colleges, churches, or temples because of stairways and other obstacles."[11] She began traveling nationwide, speaking to governors and mayors throughout the country. Because she frequently had to travel, Louise bought a car and after having hand controls installed, learned how to travel alone.

In June of 1964, La Sertoma Club delegates met for their annual International Convention in Mexico City and presented Louise with their Woman of the Year award for service to mankind. This great award served to highlight a life that had been dedicated to helping others.

Is it any wonder that Norman Vincent Peale once seated Louise in the front row of Marble Collegiate Church and spoke of her as exhibit A of the power of positive thinking? Louise Lake showed others how to live life to the fullest, not by word but by example. Wisely, Louise lived the counsel she often gave young men and women; "You will pass through this life but once! Therefore, write well your chapter, for you cannot return to rewrite it. Fill well the fullest measure of your creation, for life is eternal."[12]

Notes

1. Louise Lake, *Each Day A Bonus,* (Salt Lake City: Deseret Book, 1967), p. 12.
2. Ibid., p. 29.
3. Ibid., p. 35.
4. Ibid., p. 47.
5. Ibid., p. 54.
6. Ibid., p. 71.
7. Ibid., p. 113.
8. Ibid., pp. 120–121.
9. Ibid., pp. 122–123.
10. Ibid., p. 134.
11. Ibid., p. 182.
12. Ibid., p. 205.

Chapter 16

Max Whittier

"It's How You Finish That Counts"

In the brief second it took for the unexpected explosion to knock the soldiers off their feet, Max's world became silent. Badly injured, Max was lucky to be alive, but he felt that life had already given him more than his fair share of trials.

It was true that Max Whittier knew something about adversity. As a young boy, his family had been left penniless when the stock market crashed. Unable to draw their money out of the bank, the sheriff had come and taken away all their household belongings. It was during this bleak time that his parents had begun a tradition of having counseling sessions with their children. It was during those sessions that one of his parents' oft-repeated sayings became indelibly etched on Max's mind:

"People are not very impressed with the starts we make," they told their children. "What everybody wants to know is how we finish. . . . The most serious shortcomings of our existence are not our intentional transgressions but our inability to finish what we start."[1]

Even though his family was left destitute after the crash, Max was determined to get an education. But even though he worked and prayed hard, a college education still seemed to be beyond his grasp, until his inquisitive nature caused him to write a letter. For a long time, Max had been curious to know why sugar beet leaves often turned yellow and developed holes, even when supplied with adequate water and nutrients. Figuring the Department of Agriculture would be able to tell him the reason, he wrote and asked them about this strange phenomena. As it turned out, they didn't know either, but an entomologist was so impressed by the young man's question that he offered to pay Max $75.00 a month, which would cover all his college expenses, to work with him and discover the answer. It was a huge sum, considering that Max's father was working for only $2.00 a day.

Despite long, tiring hours and frequent failures, Max persisted and was able to pay his way through two years of college. He went on to earn a teaching certificate, then became principal at an elementary school in Ammon, Idaho.

When the Japanese attacked Pearl Harbor, Max was drafted. Feeling unhappy that he had to leave his promising new life, Max considered moving back home and getting an agricultural exemption. His two older brothers had done that and were now producing food, but when he talked with his mother, she counseled him not to apply for the exemption. Sister Whittier told her son that he had been blessed to be born into a family that belonged to the only true church on earth and that he had a responsibility to safeguard the nation that was the protector of this divine church. She promised Max that if he would honor the priesthood through his conduct, he would receive the countless blessings that he had been promised in his patriarchal blessing.

In addition, Sister Whittier cautioned her son that great adversity would be forthcoming. However, she told Max that if he was faithful to the gospel principles he had been taught, including the Word of Wisdom, a way would be opened for him to not only resume his good teaching position but to be blessed with new opportunities. Max listened soberly as his mother ended by saying that he would be made stronger by overcoming the trials and adversities that would come his way. In the end, Max decided to serve his country, but before he left, he hurriedly married a girl he had been dating and received his temple endowments.

Max was sent to the South Pacific, where the weather is nearly always hot and humid. His commanding officer was extremely antagonistic toward members of The Church of Jesus Christ of Latter-day Saints and constantly harassed the young man about his "strange underwear." At night, it was so hot that Max would soak his blanket with water, spread it out, and lie on top of it to sleep. His commanding officer delighted in coming in quietly at night, walking up to where Max was sleeping, and hitting him across his bare feet with a quirt. When the others woke, the officer would loudly laugh at Max and ridicule him for wearing garments. He said that if such clothing was supposed to be a protection, they were doing a poor job. Despite the taunts, the young soldier strictly followed his mother's counsel and adhered to gospel principles even though, during the two years he spent overseas, he didn't meet one other member of the Church.

When Max wrote his parents about how he was frequently tormented, they responded, "No matter what hardships you are required to endure, be faithful, and the Lord will bless you for it."[2]

Max's wife had a baby girl in his absence, but he was unable to get a furlough to see them. Then, in 1944, his wife wrote again, stating that she had fallen in love with another man and wanted a divorce. Later that year, on August 15, he received more distressing news. His brother, Lamar, a radioman on a B 17 bomber, had been shot down in Germany and was missing in action. Max knelt in his grief and anguish and prayed, feeling his trials were too much to bear.

"You may not truly comprehend the reason for these hardships and tragedies," his parents wrote to buoy up his spirits. "But if you will go forward faithfully doing the best you can under the circumstances, you will be blessed."[3]

Then, only one week after receiving that letter, Max's world changed forever. That morning, an unexpected explosion thundered in his ears. The impact of the blast sent him flying backwards, reeling in blood and shock. Everything was strangely quiet as Max lay in the hospital bed. The doctors managed to make him understand that, while he would recover from most of his injuries, the damage to his ears was permanent. He was now almost totally deaf. Feeling very much alone in a new bleak world of silence, Max fell deeply into depression.

Despairingly he thought about his marriage that was now over, his brother who was missing in action, and the explosion that had destroyed his ability to hear. Alone, and with no member of the Church to talk with or administer to him, Max felt desolate and isolated. It seemed that no one was really interested in him. When a chaplain who was in the field hospital learned that Max could not hear, he just shook his head and, without a single word, walked out, leaving a stricken Max to stare at his retreating back.

Bitterness filled his heart and Max began to doubt that the promises his mother had made to him would ever come true. At home, over ten thousand miles away, no one knew of his plight and, dismally, Max felt no one cared. When he was sent by hospital ship to the San Diego Naval Hospital, there was no one to meet him.

Then, a few good things began happening. The American Red Cross located a telephone with a bone conduction receiver. Because the nerves in his ears had not been destroyed, Max was able to hear through this specially designed phone. The Red Cross placed a phone call to let his parents know of his condition on October 6, 1944. Miraculously, on that same day, his brother Lamar called from New York City. Lamar had managed to thread his way safely across the fields of Germany, slipping though enemy lines until he had reached friendly Allied forces.

Max was hospitalized for several more months. During that

time, he was moved to three different facilities. In each one, the local doctors tried various techniques to restore his hearing, but each failed. Finally, at Hoff General Hospital, Max was urged to attend a class to learn lip reading. Feeling the heavy weight of self-pity, Max admitted he was not a willing patient. He was depressed about the future because he knew that with his hearing loss, he could not return to his teaching position. He was further discouraged when the therapists told him not to consider any type of public service or any occupation that required verbal or forensic skills. They advised a position as a research worker, an accountant, or any other job that did not require much communication.

Max was feeling like his life was going nowhere when the hospital was blessed with a special visitor, Helen Keller. Knowing that she was not only deaf but blind and mute as well, Max watched in astonishment as Helen was guided around the hospital beds. It seemed beyond believing that, in spite of her overwhelming handicaps, she could communicate. The extraordinary woman stopped to visit with each man.

When she came to stand beside Max's own bed, Helen asked what state he was from. Brother Whittier remained silent, knowing that she could not hear. The man accompanying Helen gently touched her to let her know that Max did not believe they could communicate. Surprised, he watched as Helen placed her fingers on his lips and her thumb on his trachea and physically urged him to answer the question. Startled, he complied. Then Helen asked him another question and then another, which he answered freely.

Full of compassion for the discouraged young man, Helen

explained that even though his hearing was gone, he could develop the talents he still possessed. She said that if he would try to do this, the Lord would bless him beyond all measure. He took her words to heart.

> "I who am blind and deaf give one hint to those who see," Helen said simply. "Use your eyes as if tomorrow you would be stricken blind. And the same method can be applied to the other senses. Hear the music of voices, the song of a bird, the mighty strains of an orchestra, as if you would be stricken deaf tomorrow, touch each object as if tomorrow your tactile sense would fail. Smell the perfume of flowers, taste the relish of each morsel, as if tomorrow you could never smell and taste again. Make the most of every sense; glory and beauty which the world in all facets of pleasure reveals to you through the several means of contact which nature provides."[4]

When she left, a deep sense of shame and embarrassment washed over Max as he recalled how obstinate and ill-tempered he had been with the doctors, nurses and others who had been trying to help him.

Suddenly, the words of his parents rang in his ears. "People are not very impressed with the starts we make; what everybody wants to know is how we finish."[5] Max saw that while Helen Keller firmly believed in enjoying life to the fullest despite a person's disabilities, he had been awash in self-pity and had refused to carry on with his life. He decided to change.

From that moment on, Max attended the lip reading

sessions willingly. He became an active participant in all activities. He persuaded the other patients to play a new game he invented where they would sit on opposite sides of the hospital room and see if they could figure out what the other group was talking about. The group studied lip movements, improving in skill until, even without the benefits of hearing, they were able to carry on long, meaningful conversations.

Finally, their instructor decided they were ready for a real test. The teacher divided them into teams of two and handed them tickets to Reno, Nevada, for the weekend. Without the help of a third party, they were to register in a hotel, order their meals and seek out people with whom to visit and socialize—all without letting anyone know they were deaf. When Max and his friend walked into a place of entertainment, they spied two ladies sitting some thirty feet distant.

One girl spoke in a whisper to her friend, "Do you suppose they are going to pick us up?" Since Max could see their faces, he easily understood what had been said.

Hurrying over, Max replied, "Sure, where would you like to go?"[6] Shocked, the girls grabbed their purses and with red faces, practically ran out of the building without giving Max an opportunity to explain.

Because Max still had ten percent of his hearing left, the doctors equipped him with a hearing aid. The aid was extremely cumbersome and consisted of a large black box that weighed approximately five pounds. He wore it under his shirt. The box was attached to an ear piece in his right ear and was powered by four D-cell batteries that he wore around his belt. Equipped with that device and with his expertise in lip reading, Max started to mingle with people once more. He decided that if Helen Keller, with all her handicaps, could associate with people, he certainly could.

Max also decided to disregard the admonition his therapists had made concerning the type of job he should be content with and filled out an application to become the manager of the United States Employment Office in Pocatello, Idaho. Although Max didn't get that particular position, he did get a job as assistant manager in Payette, Idaho. Then, after three months, he was promoted to manager of the Payette office. A short time later, he was offered a position as a rehabilitation officer for the Veteran's Administration in Boise. Max accepted and began counseling disabled veterans.

Through his counseling work, Max became acquainted with an enchanting young nurse who worked for a doctor he visited from time to time. Lucille was friendly but stern in her professional demeanor. No matter how hard Max tried to get a casual conversation going, he always met a dead end. Feeling sure Lucille was the eternal companion he had been dreaming of meeting, Max started sending her three roses each day. Although he felt she guessed who was sending them, Lucille never said a word.

Desperate, Max decided upon a dramatic scheme he hoped would sweep the lovely girl off her feet. His plan was to stop Lucille on the office steps, kneel down, tell her he loved her, and then propose. On the appointed day, just before closing time, Max went into the office. When Lucille said goodbye and started to leave, Max anxiously followed her outside. Both of them were startled when he dropped to his knees. Lucille was surprised by his actions and Max was shocked at the sound of material ripping. Horrified, Max realized that the seat of his pants had split open. His face was flame-red as he fumbled to get his suit coat off and cover himself, while Lucille stood by, laughing hysterically. Finally, she contained herself long enough to swing her long nursing cape off and throw it around him.

"Come on," she choked. "Let's go find you another pair of pants."[7]

After a period of dating, the couple was married on May 10, 1947. Although Max was content at first with his job, he began to feel frustrated when he came across questionable cases and found himself disagreeing with his supervisors interpretation of the law. Finally, Max resigned and entered law school at the University of Utah.

When the dean of the school, Spencer Kimball, noticed that Max was wearing a hearing box, he called the new student in for counseling. In his kind way, Spencer told Brother Whittier that even those who had perfect hearing found the law course to be very demanding. He wondered if he could help Max change to a profession where hearing was not so critical.

Max explained that he was aware of and had fully considered all the problems his hearing loss was going to cause. He explained that he was very proficient at reading lips and said that if he could have a seat near the front of the room, he would be quite all right. And for the parts of the lecture he would miss when professors spoke while having their backs to him while writing on the blackboard, Max resolutely declared that he would just have to study harder.

While Max was in college, Lucille worked as a head nurse at St. Mark's Hospital in order to finance her husband's schooling. However, when illness struck and she was unable to work for a time, the financial stress became so great that Max offered to quit and find a job. Lucille would not hear of it. She recited the family saying she now knew by heart: "Remember, it's not how you start, it's how you finish that people really care about."[8]

Not only did Max finish law school, he finished the four-year course in less than three years. During his last year, he served as a practitioner in the Salt Lake City Legal Aid Society, counseling indigent and handicapped people. After his graduation, he moved to Pocatello to begin practicing.

Through a set of unusual circumstances, Max began working for a senior member of the bar, Judge O. R. Baum. Working with Judge Baum not only gave him valuable experience, but also opened up many doors to Max that otherwise would have remained closed. In the coming years, he served as an assistant U.S. attorney, a city attorney in three different cities, as general counsel for the Shoshone Bannock Tribe, as an expert witness for the U.S. Senate Bureau of Indian Affairs, and as president of the Idaho Trial Lawyers. Eventually, Max started his own law firm, employing nine people. He states:

"I testify that the Lord does not break promises. If we diligently try to perform our responsibilities and duties even in the face of trails and adversity, great will be our reward and we will be made stronger. . . . My opportunity to see and be with Helen Keller was momentary . . . but she, by her example and spirit, gave my life purpose and a sense of direction that was missing until then, and by this inspirational soul taking time out of her life to touch my lips and let me know there was a way."[9]

Notes

1. Dorothy South Hackworth, *Master's Touch Volume II,* (Orem: Cedar Fort, Inc., 1988), p. 65.

2. Ibid., pp. 68–69.

3. Ibid., p. 69.

4. Ibid., p 10.

5. Ibid., p. 72.

6. Ibid.

7. Ibid., p. 76.

8. Ibid., p. 78.

9. Ibid.

Chapter 17

Curt Brinkman

"IT'S MY YEAR!"

That bright July morning in 1970 started like any other summer day in Idaho for sixteen-year-old Curtis Brinkman. Ever since he had been in seventh grade, Curtis had spent nearly every summer morning getting up at 4:30 A.M. and going to work with a crew of boys and men to move heavy irrigation pipe in the fields. Curtis was now a lean 6'7" and looking forward to playing basketball at Shelley High School that fall.

The group of boys wore rubber aprons to keep their pants dry as they moved the heavy pipes. Each section of pipe weighed about forty pounds and had to be disconnected, carried about forty feet, set in place, and then reconnected.

Curtis worked that morning alongside a friend, Tony. After they finished their field, they went to check on the water pump. The water pump was located on the crown of a hill and was fueled by a high voltage line that stood beside it. Later, Curtis tried to remember what made him decide to climb the power pole, but all he could remember was Tony telling him that he was crazy before he left to help another boy in a nearby field.

Curtis had climbed about half way up when he paused to look over the swampy area next to the pole where he and his buddies liked to play. Recently, he had caught a bunch of tadpoles there and taken them home to put in his fishpond. Curtis looked up at the huge transformers that were at least three feet in diameter and approximately twenty feet above the ground. He decided to climb beyond the transformers to the big cross members where he would be able to sit and see everything for miles. As he climbed, his rubber apron began flapping because one of the straps was broken. Curtis knew he would have to be careful to keep it clear of the lines. Once he got past the transformers, the young man marveled at how his friends looked like little toy people.

Then the wind began to blow.

The wind blew the power mainline close to his knees and then connected with the transformers, causing an arc. Curtis never knew if the arc was caused because his apron blew out and touched the wire or if it was caused by something else. All he knew was that, suddenly, the stillness of the morning was broken by a tremendous roar, brilliant flashes of light, and his own screaming.

The breaker didn't disconnect like it was supposed to and the electricity arced three times, burning itself into Curtis' body each time. His hands became fused to the pole and the electricity blew his knees apart. Then it entered his body near his groin and tore though his leg, burning a hole two inches in diameter through his left foot as it exited. When the circuit breaker finally cut off the power, Curtis fell. Mercifully, his body missed the cast iron pump below. Mark, one of the boys who was working in a nearby field, looked up to see the flashes of light. When he saw his friend fall, he started running toward the water pump. He was the first to reach Curtis who was lying face down in the swampy water. The water was steaming around Curtis' sizzling body and Mark turned him over so he could breathe.

Two boys raced to get the boss who sent for an ambulance. The Idaho Falls Hospital did not have the facilities to care for such drastic burns and sent Curtis to Salt Lake City, Utah. It took quite some time before the doctors could stabilize the badly-injured young man. Even when they did, the doctors said it would be weeks before they would know for certain whether Curtis would live or not. One thing was certain from the beginning and that was that the left leg would have to be amputated.

Curtis developed an infection, but when he was given penicillin, had an allergic reaction to it. Three days after the accident, his fever was at 105 and in order to save his life, the doctors had to amputate again, taking the left knee. Finally, it was determined that it would be necessary to amputate Curtis' right leg as well. Over a few days' time, it was necessary to pump thirty-two units of blood into the young man. Every time, Curtis had an allergic reaction to the transfusions, which caused him to develop horrible hives.

Finally the doctors told his family that the boy would live, but there were times when Curtis felt death would be preferable to the terrible, constant pain that tortured him during the day and kept him awake at night. There was operation after operation. Curtis grew to hate the whirlpool bath because he could not stop himself from screaming when the nurses would explore the open wounds in his stumps with large needles.

Recovery was slow and marked by a constant and emotionally draining round of excruciating muscle spasms, constipation, diarrhea, stomachaches, bedsores, severe itching, headaches and vomiting. Because he lived in constant pain, Curtis was often uncooperative with hospital personnel and his family. He sometimes struck out verbally at those around him and most frequently it was his family that took the brunt of his temper and complaints. It was a difficult time.

After many long months of agonizing recovery, Curtis was finally able to return home in September. That November, he went back to Shelley High School. He was careful to always lay a blanket over his lap, letting it hang down to hide the empty place where his legs should have been. But one day, Curtis' blanket failed to fool a curious little child who saw right off that the high school student had no legs and frankly asked him about it. It was an emotional shock to Curtis to realize that he was not fooling anyone with the blanket. He wondered if he had been trying to hide the loss of his legs from himself as well as from others. After that epiphany, Curtis did some soul searching and decided to stop trying to hide his handicap. However, despite his new resolve, Curtis had a difficult year adjusting to his it.

When school let out in May, Curt went to the Elks Rehabilitation Center in Boise. That summer, he met others who, like himself, had been involved in drastic accidents and now had to learn how to carve out new lives for themselves. While there, Curtis became interested in basketball and found that even though he was in a wheelchair, he enjoyed playing very much. He had a natural aptitude for the sport and was very quick on the court. It helped his spirit to belong to a team and feel useful and competent.

At the center, Curtis saw others who were much more disabled than he was. This made him appreciate all the things he still could do. One girl he particularly admired could not move anything but her head, but had learned to clench a stick between her teeth and type. She could also draw beautifully.

It was a big day when his prosthetic legs arrived. Before putting them on, Curtis had to put on an elastic "stumpsock." Then he fit his stump down into the hollow top of the leg where there was a suction plug that pushed into a hole at the knee. The pressure of the plug kept Curtis' stump inside the artificial leg.

The first time Curtis stood, he said, "This is like stilts or something. I feel like a heron."[1]

It took some time and much practice to learn how to use his new legs. It required a lot of concentration to keep his balance and for a while, Curtis was a mass of bruises and sores from his many falls. In addition, his stumps often hurt from the prosthetic legs. But he kept practicing. That summer, Curtis also learned how to drive with hand controls.

In the fall, Curtis went to Ricks College. To help pay expenses, he got a job as a resident assistant for men's housing. He became active in student government and was the assistant to the Ombudsman. In addition, Curtis was on two student government committees and co-chaired another. Besides all of that, he also was on the standards committee and remained active in his ward.

One weekend, Curtis went to a dance and sat in the balcony, talking and watching people out on the floor. Then he noticed a new girl who had especially pretty eyes and a wonderful smile. The following Sunday, he found out that the new girl was in his ward. Then, on Monday, Curtis discovered that she was also in his family home evening group. The girl with the pretty eyes was Bonnie Hymas. They went out together, enjoyed each other's company, and despite Curtis' busy schedule, began spending a lot of time together.

In April of 1974, Curtis heard about a walk-a-thon that the Primary Children's Hospital in Salt Lake City was putting on to earn money. Each participant had to secure pledges, a certain amount of money for each mile they walked. Even though it was a twenty-one mile walk, Curtis decided to try it, feeling that it would be a wonderful experience to be able to help others. Bonnie also entered. It took Curtis seven and a half grueling hours to complete the route, but when he was done, he had earned one-fourth of the total amount of money the event brought in.

Curtis continued to date Bonnie and eventually their friendship blossomed into love and they were married. Around this time, he decided to be called Curt.

Wheelchair basketball continued to interest Curt. He received encouragement from Mike Johnson, a Vietnam veteran who had lost his legs and part of his hands when a land mine had exploded. Mike was organizing a wheelchair basketball team and, because he liked the way Curt handled his wheelchair, Mike invited him to be part of the team, the first such team in Utah. During one of their games, a player from Colorado who was impressed with Curt's speed on the court, told Curt that he ought to look into para-track and field competitions. After giving it some thought, Curt sent for the necessary papers and initiated wheelchair track and field in Utah.

Curt had a natural aptitude for track and competition. He and Mike began training together with the goal of entering regional and if possible, national competition. However, finances were a problem. Curt and Mike looked for a sponsor but couldn't find one. Then, the children at Scera Park Elementary School in Orem heard about their problem. By working hard, the children managed to raise $1,193.43. Other schools donated an additional $290.00. Their generosity allowed Mike and Curt to be the first Utahns in wheelchairs to enter regional and national competition.

At the regional competition, Curt and Mike learned a lot, including the fact that their chairs were much too heavy and that most of the athletes used lightweight, trim chairs. Even though they were inexperienced, the two men won enough points to make the Western Team, which would compete in the national competition in New York City in July. During that competition, Mike wheeled away with two gold medals and Curt won two bronze medals. They did so well that they made the United States team for the 1976 Para-Olympics that was going to be held in Toronto a short time later.

During the Para-Olympics, Curt set a world record for the hundred-meter dash in a time of nineteen and seven-tenths seconds. He also took three bronze medals: one in the discus, one in lawn bowling and one in shot put. While at the Para-Olympic games in Toronto, Curt was honored to meet Bobbie Hall who was known as the father of wheelchair marathons and who was the first person in a wheelchair to enter the Boston Marathon. After they talked, Curt set two goals for himself. One was to make the U.S. team for the 1980 Olympics and one was to win the Boston Marathon.

His dream began in April of 1977 when Curt entered his first Boston Marathon. He did amazingly well and finished second. He came in three minutes behind Bobbie Hall, the man who had filled him with so much enthusiasm about the race.

Then Bonnie became pregnant and Curt was excited about becoming a father, something he had not been sure would ever happen.

In May of 1977, Curt was awarded the Golden Key Award by the governor of Utah, Scott Matheson. That July, he won the Salt Lake Deseret News Marathon in the wheelchair division. Later, the U.S. Jaycees selected him as one of the Outstanding Young Men of America.

Then, Curt decided to do something for the handicapped people in Utah County who needed transportation. He and his friend Mike decided to wheel around Utah Lake in order to raise four thousand dollars, which would buy a van to transport the handicapped. It would be a staggering one hundred and fifteen-mile long test of endurance. The furthest Curt had ever gone was forty-five miles and Mike's record was twenty-six.

The trip was more than difficult. At first Curt and Mike just had to worry about boredom, but later came rattlesnakes, dangerous drivers, cramping muscles and physical exhaustion.

Bonnie and Mike's wife, Jan, followed them in a van and, toward the end of the ordeal, tried to get their suffering husbands to quit. But the men pushed on, setting a new world record by covering one hundred and fifteen miles in only seventeen hours. The previous world record was one hundred and eight miles in five days.

That fall, Curt and Mike were the first students ever chosen to light the "Y" at Brigham Young University during a football game. It was a great honor, but Curt was even more thrilled when he and Bonnie welcomed their baby boy, Greg, into the world on September 27, 1977.

The following April, Curt had a new, lightweight chair for the Boston Marathon. However, he faced steep competition from a new contender, George Murray, who was very strong. In the end, Murray won the race, but Curt was close behind. He felt both exhausted and exhilarated to take second place with five hundred thousand people cheering him on.

Curt graduated from Brigham Young University that year and began looking for a new challenge. He found it when he decided to earn money for the Easter Seal organization by wheeling from Salt Lake City to Cedar City, a distance of two hundred and seventy-five miles, in five days. He was able to raise twelve thousand dollars for Easter Seals.

In 1978, Bonnie and Curt went to New York for the running of the New York Marathon. Unfortunately, the president of the New York Roadrunner's Club was against wheelchair competitors and tried to get a court injunction against Curt and Bobbie Hall to prevent them from participating. However, the mayor decided that the race was open to anyone who wanted to compete and he let the wheelers join. To Curt's delight, he took first place.

At his next competition, the Denver Rocky Mountain Regional, Curt received a lot of media attention and was voted the Most Outstanding Athlete.

Bonnie and Curt's second baby was born in Feb of 1979. They were happy to welcome a girl, Lorian, into their home.

When the Boston Marathon came up again, Bonnie was unable to go. George Murray, who had won the race last year, was the favorite again. The weather this year was difficult. A steady, cold rain soaked the riders and made the wheelchair rims slippery. Curt was the only racer without rubber-coated rims, which made it harder for him to grip and which also conducted the cold from the slush to his hands. During the race, his fingers began hurting so badly that he became worried about frostbite and had to pull off and ask for medical help. An ambulance was called, but after warming up a bit, Curt's fingers began feeling better and he surprised the medical crew by wheeling back onto the course and finishing the race. Despite stopping, Curt finished in seventh place. Five of the racers had to be hospitalized for hypothermia and only a few of the competitors finished.

Later that year, Curt had a blow when he discovered that he had diabetes. After spending five days in the hospital, he began taking injections every morning. He and Bonnie worked on his diet and managed to get the disease under control. While Curt was learning how to take care of his health, he continued to train hard for the Boston Marathon.

This year Bonnie came with him. Before starting the race, Curt put band-aids on each of his fingers, then checked his gloves. The sun was warm on his head when he felt a gentle touch on his shoulder. It was Bonnie. She smiled, encouraging him more than anyone else could. Then it was time to begin. He lined up and found himself on the first of three rows of wheelchair competitors. They would be given a fifteen-minute lead on the other runners.

At first, Curt was in second place behind Jim Martinsen, another racer. Then, after four miles, Curt got a stitch in his side, which steadily grew worse. In great pain, Curt had to slow down. Jim pulled away. Then George Murray passed him. Somehow, despite the agony, Curt kept going. In the distance, he saw George pass the lead racer. The race went on, mile after agonizing mile. Finally the pain began to ease and, by struggling mightily, Curt was able to catch up, then pass Jim. That only left George. He made up some time on Heartbreak Hill. Next was the Trolley Tracks, which often proved a dangerous part of the race. Curt decided to go down between them. George, however, tried to cross them. He turned too sharply and crashed.

Curt kept going, even though the cramps in his biceps were terrible. At the two-mile marker, Curt felt almost dizzy with pain. But he managed to hold on. After crossing the finish line, raised his arms high over his head, yelling, "It's my year, finally my year!"[2]

Afterwards, Bonnie told reporters, "We wanted this one so much . . . It's wonderful . . . We found out a couple of months ago that Curt has diabetes. This is the first marathon we've attempted since he's been on insulin. It's fantastic."[3]

Twenty-six-year old Curt had set a new record. His 1:55 marked the first time anyone had ever completed the 26 mile, 385 yard trek in less than two hours.

Next on Curt's agenda was the Para-Olympic games in Holland. The team of ninety-six American wheelchair athletes and their coaches left the United States on June 17. During the trip, the other athletes became better acquainted with each other and Curt let it be known that he was a member of The Church of Jesus Christ of Latter-day Saints. He conducted himself well and found that others respected his beliefs.

Curt's first race in the Olympics was the hundred-meter dash. He became worried about his heavy chair and just before the start of the race, borrowed someone else's chair. Although it didn't feel comfortable, he still managed to win the silver. The next event was the four-hundred-meter individual race and Curt took first, winning his first gold medal. He had to wait a few days until his next events, which fell on the last day of competition. The first event that day was the hundred-meter relay which the American team won, giving the young man from the United States his second gold medal. Next was lawn bowling. Although he was up against a man who had done very well in international competition, Curt beat him and won his third gold medal. Curt's last event was the four-hundred meter relay and the United States team took gold once more. At the end of the Para-Olympic Games, Curt Brinkman came home with an amazing four gold medals.

Once back in the United States, Curt had many requests for appearances and speaking engagements. Unfortunately, Curt had to turn some people down because he was busy as a member of the bishopric of the BYU 80th Ward and would not neglect his duties. Curt also had a new job as manager of a new Deseret Industries store. Still, he had a great desire to help handicapped children. He knew how hard it was for people to accept themselves when they were handicapped, but knew from personal experience that it was possible for people to rise above their disabilities. Curt said, "The biggest problem with handicapped people is getting them to accept themselves. I want to show them they can do lots of things. They just don't know what they can do until they do it."[4]

Truer words were never spoken. Curt Brinkman showed others what someone with determination could do. In a newspaper article, a reporter wrote that Curt was an angler, a camper, river-runner, horseback rider, Eagle Scout, and mountaineer. He was all of that, besides winning the Boston Marathon and winning an incredible four Olympic gold medals. Despite all his many awards, two of Curt's greatest achievements were being a husband and father. In talking about his gold medals and other achievements, Curt said, "These things are nice . . . but Bonnie is what's important,

Bonnie and Greg and Lorian. That's where my life is going. That's where my life will always, always be."[5]

Notes

1. Keith J. Karren, *The Will To Win, The Curt Brinkman Story*, (Orem: Randall Publishers, 1981), p. 69.

2. Ibid., p. 141.

3. Ibid., p. 142.

4. Ibid., p. 161.

5. Ibid., p. 163.

Chapter 18

Thomas D. Giles

THE BLIND HARPIST

Sitting in front of a large and appreciative crowd at the Beehive House in Salt Lake City, Thomas Giles stroked the thin strings of his beautifully carved harp. Angelic music wafted over the distinguished guests who had been invited to attend by President Brigham Young. Brother Giles' wonderful technique came from determined and diligent practice because he learned each new and intricate piece without the aid of written music. Of course, written music would not have helped him at all because Thomas was blind.

Thomas Davis Giles was born in 1820 in England. He began working in local coal mines when he was eight years old and continued after he grew up and his family moved to Wales. Hardworking and trustworthy, Thomas said of himself, "I always had a desire to live an honest and upright life and do my best to assist my parents."[1]

When missionaries from The Church of Jesus Christ of Latter-day Saints came to the area, they caused a great deal of excitement. The new religion was roundly criticized by leaders of other churches, especially when people began to be baptized Latter-day Saints. Soon, more than two thousand people were converted. Thomas began attending meetings with his father-in-law and joined the Church the same year that Joseph and Hyrum were killed at Carthage Jail. Thomas was baptized and confirmed on November 1, 1844.

"After they had taken their hands off my head," Thomas said later, "I instantly stood up and bore my testimony to the truth. I felt to have experienced more joy on that night than I had ever done during my life before. From thence forth, I feared God and gave Glory to him and continued to pray unto him and I received the gift of the spirit."

Excited by the witness of the truth he had received, Thomas felt a great desire to share the gospel with his friends and associates. He stated, "I was much respected by the society I formerly belonged to and I expected my testimony would be favorably received by them. Consequently I went to them and testified unto them but they would not listen to me but treated me with the greatest derision." Surprised but not daunted at their reaction, Thomas did not let their negative opinions deter him from devoting himself to his new religion.

"Notwithstanding I was not ashamed of the Gospel of Christ because I had witnessed the power of God in casting out devils, healing the sick, etc. I next went to my father and testified to the whole family. My father listened to my testimony and came with me to hear the gospel preached. After he heard, he left the Baptists and commenced to search the scriptures. My mother was greatly opposed . . . but we pervaded upon her to come and hear the preaching and shortly afterwards was baptized."[2] In the coming year, Thomas' wife, Margaret, and three of his siblings were baptized.

After being ordained a priest, Thomas began preaching locally. Seventeen months after his baptism, he was called to go on a mission. He faced much persecution. Many people threw stones thrown at him and windows were broken out in homes where meetings were held. But Thomas gained much joy by sharing the gospel.

The first man he baptized allowed the elders to hold meetings in his home, but the building was too small to accommodate the large crowds. The elders asked a tavern keeper if they could use one of the large rooms at his inn to hold their meetings. He agreed, and within a short time, the missionaries had converted not only the innkeeper but his entire family. They then decided to give up their tavern.

Thomas was impressed by many of his investigators who showed great faith. When a man in his area, William Lewis, became seriously ill, his first thought was to send for Elder Giles. Upon entering the house and finding that Brother Lewis was upstairs, Elder Giles jovially called to him. He jokingly asked what William thought he was doing by lying in bed and admonished him to get up immediately. The sick man sprang out of bed and came downstairs where Elder Giles administered to him, completely restoring his health.

On the 23rd of July in 1848, Brother Giles was moved

upon by the Spirit and spoke in tongues at the end of their Sunday meeting. The branch president gave the following interpretation: "My servant, watch, for thy life is in danger; but through thy faith thy life shall be spared."[3] Thinking the warning was for the president, Elder Giles told him to be careful.

The following Wednesday, Thomas went to work in the coal mine as usual. He was bending over when a huge piece of coal broke free from the ceiling and fell on him. Two doctors examined him. Both declared that the head injuries were so extensive that Thomas could not possibly live more than a few hours. It took some heavy persuasion on the part of family and friends to even get the doctors to clean and sew up the wounds.

Two hours passed and, to the surprise of everyone, Thomas was still alive. Three days after the accident, Elder William S. Phillips, president of the Welsh Mission, gave Thomas a blessing. After the "amen," Brother Giles got out of bed and walked a short distance. Although his eyes were irreparably damaged, the injured man continued to recover at a remarkable rate. Four weeks later, he spoke at a Church meeting. Undaunted by his loss of vision, Thomas continued to preach with a companion, Elder John Jones, who led him from place to place.

Despite his handicap, Elder Giles was made President of the Monmouthshire Conference. He began traveling extensively, visiting members, conducting meetings, baptizing, confirming and doing all he could to build the kingdom of God.

During one meeting in Southern Wales, some people became critical of the elders and declared that Mormonism had many false doctrines. Brother Giles tried to explain the various precepts so the people could understand the truth but one man called him a fool. This man, whose name was Levi, asked to have a sign of the gospel's veracity. He declared that if Thomas' religion were true and if his people were actually the people of God, then Thomas should have had his eyesight restored.

The blind man exclaimed indignantly, "If anyone ought to refrain from this work because they won't give me eyes, I ought to." Then he related that he went on to bear his testimony. "I testified to them that I knew this work was of God before I lost my sight and that I depended not for the knowledge of this work through having eyes, but through receiving the Holy Ghost and that I would rather be with this religion without one eye than with any other sect and have two eyes."[4]

In gratitude for Thomas' courageous example of faith and the service he had rendered despite his physical handicap, members throughout his conference collected enough money to purchase a harp for the blind man as a token of their love and respect. Thomas was overwhelmed when his fellow Church members presented him with the fine instrument, and he immediately began learning how to play. It was soon evident that Thomas was musically gifted. He quickly mastered the harp and became an exceptional harpist.

Then, in 1856, Thomas made the momentous decision to sail to America and settle in Salt Lake. Thirty-six year old Thomas was released as president of the Conference and he and his wife, Margaret, made preparations to leave. They crossed the ocean with their two sons, Joseph and Hyrum, aged eight and six, and a daughter Maria, aged one. They joined the Edward Bunker Handcart Company in Iowa, which was composed almost entirely of immigrants from Wales. Thomas put all his worldly possessions, except for his harp—which was sent ahead by freight—in the family's small cart. He then began pulling it across the plains following his cart partner, Alfred Reese, who led the way.

Tragedy struck when little Maria became sick and died. Further anguish came just before they reached Fort Laramie when his wife died in childbirth along with the newborn baby, Elizabeth. Because his blindness made Brother Giles unable to care for his sons, Joseph and Hyrum were sent back to the Hunt wagon train where Hannah Bowen, a widow and an old friend of the family, promised to care for them.

Even though he felt alone and worried constantly about his children, Thomas trudged on. In late September, at Martin's Hollow in Wyoming, an early storm caught the handcart pioneers near Devil's Gate. Disaster seemed imminent, especially since they had discarded all surplus supplies in an attempt to hurry on to reach the Salt Lake Valley before winter arrived because they lacked food and warm clothing. Then Thomas became ill near Fort Bridger, Wyoming, and was unable to travel. The anxious company waited two days for him to improve. However, his condition worsened and, feeling a strong sense of urgency, the pioneers decided to push forward. They left two men behind, telling them to bury

Thomas when he died, then catch up with the company.

After the company had left, Thomas was told that Parley P. Pratt was headed in their direction. Thomas took heart, feeling sure that this great man, with whom he had become acquainted with in Wales, could restore his health. In great faith, the ill man asked his two companions to administer to him—continuously if necessary—in order to keep him alive until Elder Pratt could arrive. Through remarkable faith and frequent administrations, Thomas was still alive when Parley P. Pratt reached the camp.

Elder Pratt gave a remarkable blessing. In it, he promised his sick friend "that he should instantly be healed and be made well, that he should rejoin his company and arrive safely in the Salt Lake Valley, he should rear a family and because of faithfulness he would be permitted to live as long as he wanted."[5] After the blessing, Thomas got up and, along with the two gravediggers, hurried to rejoin the company. The handcart pioneers arrived in the Salt Lake Valley on October 2, 1856.

Thomas waited anxiously for the arrival of the Hunt wagon train, which was traveling with the Martin Handcart Company. He became even more worried when reports came filtering in indicating that both were in desperate straits.

Back with the Hunt Wagon Train, Hannah and her daughter Ann did their best to look after the Giles boys in the wake of the terrible, early snowstorms. It was reported that "Hannah shared the warmth of her own body with the two little boys by wrapping them in her skirts and keeping them close to her. When relief came and the company rescued,

Hannah was found to have frozen hands and feet and a badly frosted face, but the two boys were saved."[6]

While Thomas was saddened that so many lives were lost, he nevertheless rejoiced that his sons had survived. He then asked the valiant Hannah and her daughter if they would accompany him to Ogden to be a housekeeper for his mother and sister. Hannah agreed and in time, love blossomed. A year later, Hannah and Thomas were married.

Thomas decided to use his gift with music to earn a living. Although his own harp had not yet arrived, his new friend, Brigham Young, loaned him one. The President also gave Thomas a letter of introduction that allowed him to travel freely throughout the settlements, giving concerts. Rather than charge a set admission fee, the blind man allowed people to pay whatever they could, which meant that he often was paid in wheat, produce, chickens or other goods.

"Thomas was a special favorite of President Brigham Young and was engaged by him frequently to play for important dancing parties in the old Social Hall and in the Salt Lake Theatre."[7] President Young was impressed with the handicapped man's stoic nature and unusual talent. When Thomas' harp was damaged beyond repair during a move to Salt Lake City, President Young presented him with one that had been made in his own workshop. It was a tribute to Thomas' skill that the Prophet frequently invited him to the Beehive House to play for state receptions and other important occasions.

Thomas soon gained a wide reputation as "the blind harpist." His skills were in such great demand that he and Hannah began traveling throughout Utah and even into

Southern Idaho, giving concerts and singing for dances and recitals. Besides serving people with his music, Brother Giles did what he could to help others in need. Thomas and Hannah's home in Salt Lake City became the gathering place for new Welsh immigrants. Anyone who arrived in the city without friends to meet them at the train station were taken in by the Giles family. Neighbors would pitch in to provide the newcomers with shelter and food, and if necessary, clothing, furniture and money until the new emigrants could support themselves.

Providing music soon became a family affair. Thomas's son, Henry, joined his half-brother, Hyrum, in playing the piano and violin. Joseph, Henry, and Hyrum all sang beautifully, as did their father. They gave musical performances throughout the state, with the young men driving Thomas to various cities. After a concert, chairs would be moved to the edges of the hall and dancing would follow. On one occasion in October of 1869—reportedly at the request of Brigham Young—Thomas led the Tabernacle Choir at the Weber Stake Conference.

At age eleven, young Henry had already displayed unusual musical ability. This caught the eye of Brigham Young, who said, "Brother Giles, we are going to set your boy apart as an organist. I am instructing the bishop to assign him three hymns each week. The boy is to practice them during the week."[8] Together, they laid their hands upon Henry's head and Brigham pronounced a blessing. Years later, Henry was called to open the music department for Brigham Young Academy.

Thomas ably supported his family over the years with his

magnificent performances. Through his enchanting music, the "blind harpist" provided many bright moments for his listeners. Whether his audience were dignitaries and heads of state or humble pioneers, Thomas gave everyone a powerful example of personal courage and resiliency in the face of adversity.

Notes

1. Helen Sharp Madsen, "*Thomas Davis Giles (1820–1894) of Blaenavon, Monmouthshire, England [n.d.]*," (Salt Lake City: LDS Church Archives), p. 2.

2. Ibid.

3. Ibid.

4. Ibid., p. 3.

5. Ibid.

6. Dorothy Pratt Giles Topham, "*Thomas Davis Giles and Hannah Evans Biographical Sketch 1950*," (Salt Lake City: LDS Church Archives), p. 2.

7. Ibid., p. 3.

8. Helen Sharp Madsen, "*Thomas Davis Giles (1820–1894) of Blaenavon, Monmouthshire, England [n.d.]*," op cit., p. 5.

Chapter 19

Joseph C. Bentley

ESCAPE WAS IMPOSSIBLE

Killing, looting, burning homes, robbing farms—all these crimes were committed by Pancho Villa, a rebel leader during the Mexican Revolution. General Villa became bitter toward Americans when the United States government recognized Pancho's enemy, Carranza, as the legitimate President of Mexico and cut off Pancho's supplies.

At this time of war and upheaval, Joseph Charles Bentley and his wife, Gladys, were living in the Mormon colony of Colonia Juarez. One day, word came to the small town that General Villa and his army had been sighted thirty miles west of the village. Everyone was terrified to know that the infamous outlaw was so close, particularly as all avenues of escape had been cut off. Their horses had already been stolen, the railroad was destroyed, and there were no automobiles. In addition, the entire area was crawling with thieves and bandits, which meant that anyone who tried to venture out of the tiny village and tried to cross the countryside to reach the United States would be committing suicide.

However, General Villa was not headed for Colonia Juarez. He was going to the American border because he was running low on food and ammunition. When he reached Columbus, New Mexico, Villa encountered a troop of American soldiers who attacked his band. Villa's men retreated quickly, but many were wounded or killed. Angry about the defeat and frustrated at being unable to obtain the desperately needed supplies, Pancho and his men rode away in a bitter mood. Turning south, they decided to head for Colonia Juarez.

To boost the men's spirits after the humiliating skirmish, General Villa announced that when they reached the settlement, they would be allowed to plunder, steal, and loot to their hearts' desire. The general placed only one condition upon his men: when they had finished pillaging and destroying, the soldiers were to kill everyone and burn the town to the ground. They were commanded to leave no witnesses.

As president of the stake, Joseph Bentley regularly sent out scouts to watch General Villa's troops and report on their movement. It was early on a Sunday morning when the scouts returned with frightening news. Pancho Villa and his troops had gone through the north pass and were heading in their direction. They would be in Colonia Juarez by sunrise. The entire town was in shock, knowing that escape was virtually impossible. Most believed they would be dead soon after dawn. Frantic mothers tried to hide their children in the river bottoms by covering them with sand and dead branches. Others hid in trees or other places that offered scant protection.

President Bentley strode about the village, visiting the frightened members and offering assistance and comfort. That night, he stayed up praying and watching. When morning finally came, he walked alone through the quiet town, his senses alert, surprised that the soldiers had not yet arrived. Hours went by. Finally at noon, he ordered the scouts to go and discover the location of Villa's troops.

The scouts returned with miraculous news. They reported that although Villa and his army had come to the edge of the colony, they had suddenly and sharply turned and gone east. The scouts had followed them for some distance to make sure they were really gone before returning to Colonia Juarez. No one could understand why Villa had suddenly veered away, but everyone offered thanks to Heavenly Father for protecting them from harm. Quite some time passed before President Bentley learned why Villa had not attacked the helpless colony that day.

In the interim, Elder Bentley was called to serve as president of the Mexican Mission. One evening he and a young companion, Elder Whetten, were traveling through the countryside, visiting the wards and branches. They had set up camp for the night by a spring when three soldiers rode up. After finding out who the two men were, the soldiers told President Bentley that General Villa wanted to see him. The men did not resist and were taken to the leader's headquarters where they were kept for nine days. Although Elder Bentley and

Elder Whetten were not allowed to leave, they were treated cordially and given the best treatment they could hope for under such conditions.

When President Bentley had an opportunity to meet with General Villa, he could not help but ask the question that had been on his mind for so long. Why, on that long ago day, had General Villa come so close to Colonia Juarez and then pulled away instead of attacking?

Looking contemplative, Pancho pondered the question deeply. "Mr. Bentley," he replied pensively, "that is one thing I have never been able to understand myself. It might interest you to know that when we got to the edge of those colonies, a great vision opened up before me, and instead of seeing those colonies as I remembered them, I could see the houses all right, but they were all in flames. I can see that picture now—those homes burning—and I felt that the heat would be so terrific that it would be unsafe for me and my army with our wounded men to even venture near."

He continued, "The surprising thing was that none of the men saw the same picture that I saw, and when I gave them the command to turn aside and march around the colonies, taking our wounded soldiers with us, many of them were very resentful and reminded me of my promise, but I turned to them and said, 'Can't you see the colonies are already on fire? It would be dangerous for us to go in!' But they couldn't see it. Because they couldn't, it angered me and I gave the command that any man who didn't obey orders should be shot.

"We marched on and it wasn't until we had gone miles that I came to realize that perhaps I had been mistaken and maybe those colonies weren't on fire. I turned around and looked toward them, but I could see nothing, yet I felt we were too far away to turn back, so we continued on."

Pancho paused a few moments. "No, Mr. Bentley, I have never been able to understand it to this day, because I have learned since that those colonies were not on fire—that not a single home was burned, and yet I saw that picture as vividly as I see you standing in front of me."[1]

Notes

1. V. W. Bentley, in Faith Promoting Stories, compiled by Preston Nibley, (Salt Lake City: Deseret Book Company, 1943), pp. 58–59.

Chapter 20

Karl Schnibbe & Helmuth Huebener

TELLING PEOPLE THE TRUTH

As Adolf Hitler slowly rose to power, prior to World War II, his regime's point of view underwent a dramatic and deadly transformation. At first, their stance was that people should take great pride in their country, but soon their way of thinking changed and the Nazis became obsessed with a fanatical belief that the German people were superior to all others.

Along with other members of The Church of Jesus Christ in Germany, two teenagers, Karl Schnibbe and Helmuth Huebener, watched as Hitler's power increased and his dark doctrine was slowly revealed. When the evil that was inherent in the Nazi regime became blatantly obvious, the two young men felt compelled to do what they could to fight its diabolical influence.

When he was a young boy, Karl-Heinze Schnibbe had joined the newly-organized Nazi Youth Party, which was, in the beginning, an innocent, patriotic organization. But as time went on, the organization slowly changed, becoming militant in nature and prejudiced against Jews. When Karl realized that the group was becoming more like the Gestapo than the public-spirited club it used to be, he dropped out.

As Hitler stepped up his propaganda, matters worsened. Karl never forgot the day he walked past the office of his family doctor who was also a dear friend of his family. There was a "Closed" sign displayed on the door, even though it had been open the day before. Horrified, he knew exactly what had happened. Dr. Caro, a gentle man who had delivered Karl into the world, had been taken silently away to be disposed of because he was a Jew.

Karl and Helmuth Huebener were both active and well-liked in their Latter-day Saint branch but Helmuth was the natural leader. He always knew the answer whenever a question was asked in his Sunday School, Priesthood, or MIA classes. He enjoyed intellectual discussions and had a ready wit. When Helmuth's mother got married again—to a rabid Nazi—Helmuth and his siblings went to live with his grandparents because none of them could stand the rigid fanaticism of their new stepfather.

Hitler's bitter persecution of the Jews continued to shock the boys who were outraged to see them treated so mercilessly. They felt the Nazis' iron-clad laws deprived not only the Jews but all people of freedom and liberty. Helmuth, especially, felt it was morally wrong to sit idly by, doing nothing, while this evil tide flooded his country.

Helmuth's first act of resistance was to get a small radio. With it, he could hear the nightly broadcasts of the British Broadcasting Corporation. Listening to these transmissions was against the law, but Helmuth felt it was the only way he could learn the truth about what was actually happening in the war. He suspected, as many Germans did by then, that what the Nazis told the people was mostly lies or selected bits of truth mingled with flagrant propaganda. The radio became his tie to the truth.

It was in the summer of 1941, when the war was in full swing, that Helmuth first invited Karl over to listen to his radio. They couldn't always pick up the signals, as the Nazis tried nightly to jam the broadcasts, but Helmuth was quick to point out to Karl that the Wehrmachtsbericht—the military press releases announced by the Nazis—were all lies. In the coming months, Helmuth invited other boys to come and listen to the Nazi broadcasts. Over a period of time, they heard the Germans announce the sinking of a British aircraft carrier, the Ark Royal, three separate times.

Soon, Helmuth wanted to do more than invite other boys to come and listen to the radio. He and Karl felt the public needed to hear the truth about what was really going on. He felt that if his fellow Germans knew the Nazis were lying to the people, they would resist Hitler's sordid plans and stop following the dictator so blindly.

It would be too slow as well as dangerous to talk to people individually and let them know the truth. So Helmuth came up with an idea. He and Karl would distribute handwritten leaflets containing truths gleaned from the illegal English broadcasts. By using the leaflets, the boys felt they could reach the masses rather than just a few selected friends and family members. At the end of the leaflet, readers were asked to pass them on.

Even though distributing the leaflets was risky, Helmuth persuaded another boy, Rudi Wobbe, to join them in their resistance efforts. Karl, Helmuth and Rudi knew that if they were caught, they would face terrifying consequences, yet they felt a moral responsibility to fight Hitler's evil influence. Because fear of being discovered was an ever-present worry, the boys agreed that if one of them got caught, they would not incriminate the others but would take all the blame upon themselves.

At first, Helmuth laboriously wrote out all of the leaflets by hand but that process proved to be too slow. In the branch, Helmuth worked as a clerk to President Soellner. Because of his secretarial duties, he had a key to the branch meetinghouse. Since he also had permission to take the branch's typewriter to his home, he borrowed it and used carbon paper to speed up production of the leaflets.

Helmuth asked Karl to help him distribute the fliers once every two weeks. Soon, however, they began passing them out once a week, then twice a week. The boys put them on apartment houses, in phone booths, anywhere they could leave them anonymously. It was too dangerous to pass them directly to another person. Even having one in your possession could result in an arrest.

It wasn't long before Helmuth decided to increase the production of leaflets once again. He began using the branch's duplicating machine and eventually composed sixty different leaflets. On the leaflets, he would write his belief that Hitler was not telling the truth and go on to explain exactly why. Helmuth recruited others to help distribute his leaflets and to listen to the facts on the BBC. The boys hoped the leaflets would cause a chain reaction of discussion and that more and more people would become so angry and indignant over the lies that they would revolt against Hitler's wicked plans.

One day, Helmuth learned that some French prisoners of war were incarcerated nearby. He decided to distribute leaflets among them. But first, the leaflets needed to be translated into French. Helmuth knew that a coworker of his, Werner Kranz, spoke French. The boy approached Kranz at work to ask if he would do the translating. Their whispered conversation aroused the suspicions of Heinrich Mohns, a fellow worker and overseer, who was loyal to the Nazis. Mohns later questioned Kranz, then Gerhard Duewer, another of Helmuth's recruits. When Mohns found an incriminating leaflet on Gerhard, he promptly notified the Gestapo.

On February 5, 1842, Helmuth was arrested and his apartment searched. The Gestapo found the typewriter, carbon copies, a radio, leaflets, and notes. They had an ironclad case for treason. Secrecy was so fundamental to the Nazis that it was days before Karl found out that Helmuth had been arrested. Karl then spent the next few days in an agony of fear and apprehension.

On February 10th, Karl was at work painting an apartment

when two men in soft felt hats and long leather coats appeared. After many questions, they arrested Karl and took him to his home, which they searched thoroughly. To protect his family, Karl had always been careful never to leave anything incriminating there, so the Gestapo found nothing. However, he was still taken to prison. His family, who had not been home at the time of the search, didn't find out about his arrest until weeks later. Karl later found out that Rudi Wobbe had been arrested the same day and that Gerhard Duewer was also in prison.

The next three weeks followed a harrowing routine. Every morning, Karl was taken to Gestapo headquarters for questioning. Along with sixty other men, he stood for hours with his nose pressed against the wall, the preferred position for prisoners. The room the men stood in while waiting to be interrogated was called the room of mirrors. It was called that because the room was painted a glossy white and was lit so brilliantly that after the prisoner had stood for long hours, it had a dizzying effect on them. While waiting, the men would often become disoriented, lose their balance and fall, only to be pummeled by vicious kicks from the SS men who guarded them.

On one of Karl's first falls, an SS man kicked at him and snarled, "So, you wanted to bring Germany to fall—and now you are the one who is falling, right?"[1]

Karl prayed every ten minutes to have the strength to endure. Once, when he was in the room of mirrors, he caught a glimpse of Helmuth whose bruised and puffy face testified that he had been badly beaten. Unfortunately, there was no opportunity to communicate with each other.

The questioning went on day after day in an attempt to find out the names of the older men the Nazis believed were behind Helmuth's remarkably effective resistance campaign. The Gestapo simply refused to believe that a sixteen-year-old boy could have masterminded such a widespread resistance plot.

Finally, the soldiers transferred the boys to another prison. There, the young men faced a new psychological terror. Their cells were directly above death row and every day, there were between five and fifteen executions. Some of the men went calmly, others went screaming, but each one was torture to Karl. Finally, the authorities notified Karl's parents of his arrest. They were allowed to visit him for five minutes once a month.

After Karl had spent six months in prison, a guard gave him documents that contained the official charges against him. They included conspiracy to commit high treason and treasonous aiding and abetting of the enemy. His heart sank when he read that his case was to be tried before the Volksgerichtshof, which was the most feared court in all Berlin. It was well known that the majority of the people tried there were sentenced to death.

After receiving the charges, Karl was sent to Alt-Moabit prison and kept in solitary confinement. When the trial began, the prosecutors concentrated their efforts on Helmuth. He was the instigator of the resistance plot and freely acknowledged his activities. Karl watched as Helmuth stood firm as an oak before the Nazi inquisitioners, calmly answering all their questions. He even told about listening to the truth on the BBC.

"Do you mean to tell us that British stories are the truth?" an astounded Nazi bellowed.

Without hesitation, Helmuth answered, "Exactly."

When they asked Helmuth why he distributed the leaflets, he replied simply, "Because I wanted people to know the truth."[2]

Finally, the trial ended. Gerhard Duewer had been charged with listening to the British broadcasts but denied it. Although the Nazis had no proof that he had actually listened to the radio, he was sentenced to four years in prison. Karl was sentenced to five years of hard labor, but was forced to spend seven years working. Rudi Wobbe was sentenced to ten years, partly because he had talked to an informant who had been planted in his prison cell. Helmuth, the leader of the resistance plan, was sentenced to execution by guillotine.

Before leaving the courtroom, Helmuth turned and faced his accusers. "You kill me for no reason at all. I haven't committed any crime. All I've done is tell the truth."[3]

As the boys left the courtroom, the onlookers rose to their feet in respectful silence. Some stood as a salute to Helmuth's courage, others in awe that not all the boys had been sentenced to death. The young men were taken to the basement where they read heart-rending notes previous prisoners had scratched on the thick walls. Most of the writers simply stated their name and the fact that they were sentenced to die.

While there, Karl was granted a two-minute visit with his

father. After his father left, Karl tried to cheer up Helmuth, telling him that his lawyer would be sure to appeal the decision to another court. However, when his friend stepped out of the room, Karl knew deep in his heart that he would never see Helmuth again in this life. It was apparent that Helmuth felt the same way for his last goodbye was spoken very solemnly.

Karl, Rudi, and Gerhard were each transferred to different prisons. Weeks went by and appeal after appeal for Helmuth was denied. Hope finally ran out.

Before his execution, the officials asked Helmuth for his last request. He asked to write three letters, one to his mother, one to his grandmother, and one to Sister Sommerfeld, a lady who had treated him like a son. A few months later, Helmuth's mother and grandmother were killed in a bombing raid and their letters were destroyed, but the letter to Sister Sommerfeld survived:

Dear Sister Sommerfeld and Family,

When you receive this letter, I will be dead. But before my execution I have been granted one wish, to write three letters to my loved ones. I want to thank you for the letter you sent to me, dear Sister Sommerfeld, which they withheld from me. I also want to thank you for the many happy hours I was able to spend in the circle of your family. Please remember me kindly. I am very thankful to my Heavenly Father that this agonizing life is coming to an end this evening. I could not stand it any longer anyway! My Father in Heaven knows that I have done nothing wrong. I am only sorry that in my last hour I have to break the

Word of Wisdom. I know that God lives and He will be the proper judge of this matter.

Until our happy reunion in that better world, I remain,

Your friend and brother in the gospel

Helmuth[4]

On October 27th, Helmuth was forced to drink wine to dull his senses. He regretted it but had little choice. He was then led to the execution room and his life was ended. After his death, the Nazis feared an uprising because of Helmuth's tremendous popularity. To counteract this possibility, they printed hundreds of leaflets full of propaganda, announcing the death of a traitor.

"It was clear," Karl wrote later, "that the Nazis feared the truth more than they feared weapons, and leaflets more than guns."[5]

Karl himself went though innumerable trials and sufferings in various concentration camps. It wasn't until April of 1949 that he was finally released from a Russian camp. Although he returned home feeble and emaciated, he was a hero in the eyes of all who knew him.

Notes

1. Blair R. Holmes & Alan F. Keele, (compiled, edited, translated) *When Truth Was Treason,* (Chicago: University of Illinois Press, 1995), p. 55.

2. Karl-Heinz Schnibbe, with Alan F. Keele and Douglas F. Tobler, *The Price,* (Salt Lake City: Bookcraft, 1984), p. 52.

3. Ibid., p. 54.

4. Blair R. Holmes & Alan F. Keele, *When Truth Was Treason,* op cit., p. 240.

5. Karl-Heinz Schnibbe, with Alan F. Keele and Douglas F. Tobler, *The Price*, op cit., p. 56.

Chapter 21

Belton Palmer

"THERE IS NOTHING IMPOSSIBLE"

Duffy and Belton Palmer were unusually close brothers. In fact, many people mistook them for twins. When Duffy joined the marines, Belton decided to go with him and they made a pact never to leave one another. Then Duffy was promoted to sergeant and, because of marine tradition, the two were separated. However, just before the marines landed on Iwo Jima, their request to be put back in the same company was granted. So it was that the two brothers were together when they faced the most dangerous mission of their lives.

At that time, the Japanese had a firm hold on the island of Iwo Jima and, even though it seemed nearly impossible to dislodge them, the Marine Corps were commanded to regain control of the island. When the elite corps of marines first hit the beaches, they were pelted by fierce enemy fire. Duffy had been ordered to get his men up the hill and he encouraged them to slowly work their way up by running from one protective shell-hole to another. Heavy enemy fire made it an excruciatingly slow process. It seemed that Duffy was drawing an extra amount of attention from Japanese guns.

One corporal complained, "Duffy, I am going to drop back. They are after you." The corporal moved his men away, but three days later, returned. Contritely, he asked if his squad could dig in by the sergeant. Surprised, Duffy asked why he had changed his mind. The corporal responded, "If ever a man's life is charmed, yours is."

Duffy pondered his comrade's comment, then decided, "No, not charmed, but guided and blessed by one higher, oh much higher than I."[1]

The battle raged on and Duffy continued to lead his group painstakingly up the slope. He and another soldier were a few yards ahead of their unit when a mortar shell landed nearby. The terrific force from the shell blasted a massive shower of dirt over Duffy, almost completely burying him. The marine next to him was killed instantly.

Stunned and unable to move, Duffy watched as the platoon sergeant crawled over and picked up the dead marine's rifle. The sergeant looked over at Palmer and dismally shook his head, obviously thinking that Duffy had also been killed. When the platoon sergeant returned to the line, Belton asked if his brother was all right. The sergeant didn't have the heart to tell him that his brother was dead, so replied instead that he thought so.

After a while, Duffy recovered his senses enough to crawl

out from under the dirt into the huge new hole the mortar had carved out in the earth. When he looked over the edge of his hole toward his outfit, he saw Belton waiting for his okay signal, which he gratefully gave.

The battle continued. Every night and morning and many times in-between, the brothers would lie in the foxholes, clasp hands, and pray to Heavenly Father for wisdom, strength, courage, and protection. Often, they felt the Lord's hand protecting them from harm.

When Duffy received orders to move his group forward twenty-five yards, he decided to go ahead to check out the area. He cautioned his men to hold their positions until he motioned for them to come. Duffy then jumped out of his foxhole and ran frantically, searching for a nearby hole. His heart raced with fear when he saw there were none within his preferred range. The closest one was fifty yards away and he dove into it full tilt, thankful to have made it there alive.

However, it was unthinkable to have his men come that way and he peered over the edge of the hole to signal his men to stay put. As Duffy raised his head to warn his men, he was showered with enemy fire. Bullets entered his neck, back and chest. Frantically he tried to call out for help, but no sound came. Duffy knew he was hit bad, but was unwilling to die. Unable to turn to others for help, he turned to Heavenly Father and prayed for his life.

When the Lord momentarily restored his voice, his first words were, "No God, not now."[2]

Belton sensed that his brother was in trouble, but when he jumped up to run to Duffy's aid, his lieutenant pulled him back down. The lieutenant said it wasn't possible to help Duffy without getting hit himself. Even as the lieutenant's words rang in Belton's head, the tremendous devotion Belton had for his brother proved stronger. No power on earth could stop him from going to Duffy's aid. All during this long battle, Belton had watched over and protected Duffy. He had covered him with rifle fire as he moved from foxhole to foxhole. He had given orders and encouraged his men at critical times. He wasn't about to give up on his brother now.

Unconcerned about his own safety, Belton leaped up and started up the hill. Bullets bit into the dirt at his feet as the Japanese tried to cut him down. Miraculously, he arrived safely at Duffy's foxhole. One look, however, was enough to tell him that his brother was in bad shape. Tearing his bloodied shirt off, Belton administered first aid as best he could. Then he anointed his brother with oil and gave him a priesthood blessing. Although Belton had done all he could, he knew that his brother needed medical help if he was going to survive. That meant Belton would have to go back through the fierce hail of gunfire to the main group and return with a medical corpsman if Duffy's life was to be saved.

Somehow, Belton made it back to his group and, just as miraculously, he returned safely with a corpsman who tended to Duffy's wounds and gave him plasma. The next thing was to get his injured brother back to the main group where he could get more sophisticated medical attention. But carrying Duffy would slow them down tremendously. He would need to have the marines cover them if Duffy were to be moved safely. That meant another trip to tell the soldiers what to do.

Belton continued to defy the odds and the Japanese guns by returning yet again. He told the marines to open fire when he and the corpsman carried Duffy out. The marines did their part, shooting furiously as Belton and the corpsman carried Duffy down the dangerous hillside and through a rain of bullets to safety.

Duffy lived—because of a brother who loved him enough to risk his own life. Belton said later that he believed the one reason he was in the Marine Corps was to save Duffy's life. But how was he able to accomplish such a seemingly impossible task?

"There is nothing impossible when God has his protecting arm around you,"[3] Duffy answered simply. His brother is living proof that God had his sheltering arm around two brothers on the war-torn island of Iwo Jima.

Notes

1. "Letter to Lt. Com. John W. Bond," *Deseret News, Church Section*, 7 July 1945, p. 9.

2. Ibid.

3. Ibid., p. 12.

Chapter 22

Elder Monrov

"I CANNOT DENY THE GOSPEL"

Pulling the missionaries out of Mexico was an agonizing decision but President Joseph F. Smith had little choice. Violence from opposing northern and southern factions had escalated during the Mexican War, making it too dangerous for the missionaries to stay. In 1913, President Smith sent a message to Elder Ray Pratt, the mission president, that he and his missionaries would have to leave the area. They sent word of their imminent departure to all the branches.

The missionaries were concerned about leaving members of the Church who were relatively new in the faith and looked to them for guidance, so they wrote lengthy farewell messages to the members. Among other things, they expressed their hope that their teachings would be sufficient to enable the people to take care of themselves.

Elder Pratt was packing his belongings when a young man, Brother Monrov, accompanied by his wife, mother, and three neighbors, came to the mission home. Brother Monrov had been baptized only two months previously and looked sorrowful as he clasped Elder Pratt's hand.

"Brother Pratt, is it true that you are going away? Is it true that the missionaries are going to leave us?"

"Yes, Brother Monrov. It seems that is the wisest thing to do."

"Well, I have been around and visited the other conferences and branches some and I know that they have their branch organizations and their conferences and the priesthood of the Lord and they can get along in some sort of way, but what is going to become of us? We have no branch. Who will teach us? Who will guide us? Who will carry us forward in this great work?"

Elder Pratt clasped his friend's arm, looking thoughtfully into his dark eyes. Then he indicated a chair. "Dear brother, please sit down." After the young man had done so, Elder Pratt stepped out of the room and asked Elder Young, the secretary of the mission, to come in.

"Brother Young," he began, extending a hand toward Brother Monrov. "We will ordain this good brother an elder and set him apart to preside over the branch in San Marcos, though there are perchance only ten people there who are members of the Church."

After the ordination, Elder Pratt counseled the stunned new leader: "Brother, you go back up there and gather your little branch of people together and tell them of this. We have not time to go and tell them about it." Then he gave the new leader further counsel. "You take care of them as best you can, put your faith and trust in the Lord and He will bless you and magnify you and you will be an instrument for good in that community."[1]

That night, Brother Monrov took his family and friends to the train and returned home to begin his new responsibilities. Months passed. Elder Pratt regularly received letters from the young man that were full of faith and devotion to the Lord and full of love toward his fellowman.

The spreading revolution eventually reached Elder Monrov's hometown of San Marcos. Suddenly, the Saints found themselves living on the firing line between the northern and southern factions. The faithful members continued to attend their meetings, although occasionally, the speaker had to pause as shells whistled over the meetinghouse. Despite the tumult caused by war, sixty new members were baptized as a direct result of Elder Monrov's unremitting labors. One year after the missionaries had left, the number of people regularly attending the branch had risen from ten members to nearly one hundred.

Eventually, the weaker northern faction gave way and was driven out of the area. Shortly after, the people were frightened to see men from the southern band—who were led by a man named Zapata—arrive to inspect San Marcos. Zapata's soldiers were well-known political fanatics who believed it was not only their right, but their sworn duty to exterminate anyone whose thinking deviated from their own narrow point of view.

As the soldiers galloped triumphantly into town, they stopped to question a man who had been walking down the dusty road. The man apprehensively studied the hardened faces of the heavily-armed group. Anxious to divert the soldiers' attention from himself, he pointed nervously at a group of men further down the road.

"There is a man over there who has been assisting the people of the other faction. He has been a colonel in the other army."[2] He gave a full description of the man the soldiers should look for and quickly scurried off. They rode on to find the man who had been described so carefully—Elder Monrov.

The soldiers maneuvered their horses into a close circle, surrounding the unsuspecting man and a friend who was with him. When the soldiers asked if he had a store of arms, Elder Monrov replied with a startled "No." Then, after thinking a moment, he reached into his pocket and drew out a Bible and a Book of Mormon.

"These are my arms," he said thoughtfully. "I have carried and I (do) carry them to benefit, not to destroy my fellow-men."[3]

The rough soldiers arrested Elder Monrov and the other young man. Taking them to a nearby tree, they uncoiled their ropes and strung both men up until they fainted. The unconscious men were then lowered to the ground. When they had revived, the gruff soldiers again demanded to know where they had hidden the firearms.

While this was happening, other soldiers were going through the village, asking questions. When they returned to the main group, they reported that many of the people in San Marcos were members of a curious religion and that Elder Monrov was largely responsible for their embracing this peculiar sect. They then accused the young man of teaching a strange religion about strange gods and of unduly influencing the people of the community. They demanded that he renounce his teachings.

"I cannot do it," he replied soberly, "for I know that what I have received is true and I cannot renounce my religion."[4] The soldiers threw the two men into jail. Even in prison, Elder Monrov continued his missionary efforts and he began teaching the gospel to the other prisoners.

When Elder Monrov's sisters heard of his arrest, they went immediately to see the general. When they begged to have their brother released, the impatient leader ruthlessly threw the women into jail as well.

That evening, his widowed mother sent a package of food to the little adobe house for her children. Elder Monrov received it gratefully, then asked for water. The guards watched in surprise as he combed his hair, then washed himself, cleaning his neck gingerly around the rope burns. They continued to stare as he and his sisters spread out the food.

"If you have no objections," Elder Monrov said to the curious onlookers, "we would like to ask the blessings of the Lord upon this food." After the prayer, he took his sisters aside and spoke quietly. "I will not eat tonight. I am fasting and praying to the Lord."[5]

Ten minutes later, a group of solders came to get the two men. The sun had just fallen below the western horizon. In its fading light, Elder Monrov and his friend were pushed against a great ash tree. Six soldiers lined up opposite them, holding their rifles. The general stepped forward.

"Now, as one last chance, we tell you if you will renounce your religion and confess before the Virgin Mary, we will forgive you and we will save your lives."

Elder Monrov searched his heart for several long, silent moments. "Gentlemen, I cannot, for I know what I have taught and what I have accepted is the gospel of Jesus Christ."

"All right, then prepare yourself, but have you anything to say before you are executed?"

"Yes, I will make one last request, that I be permitted to kneel here and pray." In his prayer, he asked the Lord to bless his widowed mother and to provide for her. He also asked for a blessing upon his wife and his little child that he would be leaving. Then he asked for a blessing to be upon the branch of the Church for which he was responsible.

"Lord, bless this little flock that they may not go astray, but that someone will be raised up to lead them." Then he turned toward the soldiers. "Lord, forgive these men, for they know not what they do."

Rising, he folded his arms. "Gentlemen, I am at your service."[6] Moments later, his sisters in the small adobe jail and his mother who was a quarter of a mile away, heard the roar of the guns that ended his life.

After learning of the incident, Elder Ray Pratt declared,

"What was it that took that man, smiling and with faith like that, to his execution? It was none other than that same testimony that Joseph Smith bore to the world to the very day that he sealed his testimony with his blood."[7]

Notes

1. Rey, P. Pratt, "His Faith," *Deseret News, Church Section,* 1 December 1934, p. 3.

2. Ibid.

3. Ibid.

4. Ibid.

5. Ibid.

6. Ibid., pp. 3, 8.

7. Ibid., pp. 8.

Chapter 23

The Missionary Soldier

ONE MAN'S LOVE

When the United States officially declared war against Germany, missionaries in that country were called home. Later, some of them returned, but this time they were not dressed in white shirts and ties but in soldier's khaki—supposedly enemies to a people they had once loved and served.

One elder returned to the land of his missionary labors as a corporal assigned to a reconnaissance group. His job was to go out on advance patrol. From the information he gathered, he was to select the best routes for attack. Sadly, he eyed the familiar streets and towns where he had tracted not so long ago. The streets were now neglected and torn apart by the ravages of war.

A pervading sense of unhappiness shrouded him. One factor contributing to his melancholy was a sense of isolation.

He simply did not fit in with the other soldiers. As a member of The Church of Jesus Christ of Latter-day Saints, some of his principles were different from his comrades. Although the other men were smilingly amused when they discovered that he neither smoked nor drank, his sergeant was outright disdainful. This rough, macho-type officer viewed the elder with open contempt because he did not drink, curse, or carouse with women. Although no direct confrontation had yet occurred, his superior clearly considered him a sissy and the two were often at odds.

One afternoon, the young man came upon a group of ragged, local people who were being arrested for looting. In war-torn countries, poor people in desperate circumstances were often forced to choose between scavenging or watching their families starve to death. The young corporal greatly pitied those who were trapped in such a situation. As he looked over the pinched faces, he was astonished to see a familiar, wrinkled face in the crowd. Seeing an old friend reminded the young man of happier times and he brushed past his sergeant in a hurry to reach the elderly man. They greeted each other with cries of joy and hugged each other affectionately.

Furious at this unseemly behavior, the sergeant grabbed the corporal's arm and pulled him away. Undaunted, the young man excitedly explained that before the war, he had been a missionary and taught this particular man the gospel. The corporal added that this elderly fellow was the only person he had baptized and that he knew him to be a good man. The sergeant felt that his authority was being challenged and became livid. He was also keenly aware that the other soldiers were watching closely to see what he would do.

"Insubordination, corporal?" he shouted with a hard look on his face. "This man was caught looting and apparently you need a lesson in loyalty. Okay. Early tomorrow morning he will be shot—and you'll be doing the shooting!"[1]

The young soldier blanched, then refused. The sergeant couldn't believe his ears. His authority was being deliberately challenged, and in front of his unit! He would not stand for it.

"Let me understand you, corporal," he spoke in a low voice that was hard as steel. "Are you disobeying a direct command in time of war? If so, it's my duty to remind you that that's an offense punishable by death. We're moving fast, and I'm the law out here. We don't have time for a court martial. You have until morning to make up your mind. At five in the morning that looter will be staring down the muzzles of a firing squad. You'll either be on the business end of a rifle, or you'll be standing beside your friend. Take your choice."[2]

Turning on his heel, he strode away angrily, leaving the young soldier staring after him in shock. Surely, the officer couldn't be serious. Then again, he knew how ruthless the sergeant could be.

The former missionary spent a sleepless night deeply examining his beliefs. At times he wondered if the sergeant was bluffing, yet at other times, felt sure the threats would indeed be carried out. But no matter whether the sergeant meant it or not, he always ended up with the same conclusion. There was no way he could take the life of a good man whom he had personally led into the waters of baptism.

The next morning, the sergeant assembled his company of men with the looters. Bringing the corporal to the front, he ordered him to shoot his elderly friend. When the young man refused, he ordered the corporal to stand beside the elderly man in the middle of a lonely field. There, the old man and the missionary who had taught him the gospel were shot down. "Greater love hath no man than this, that a man lay down his life for his friends." (John 15:13.)

Notes

1. Kris Mackay, *No Greater Love,* (Salt Lake City: Deseret Book, 1982), p. 4.

2. Ibid.

Chapter 24

The Young Marine

Against All Odds

Just before dawn, huge battleships lined up against the horizon of the blue Pacific—waiting. Soon, the signal would come and the day's battle would begin as the Americans attempted to take the Marshall Islands. The battleships weren't the only ones poised for action on that vast ocean. Further toward shore, other boats lay waiting, smaller ones filled with marines. After the battleships bombarded the land with shells, the soldiers in the diminutive boats would row toward the island and attack the land with their own bodies, wading through the final stretch of water as they faced the fire of enemy machine guns.

The sky was a murky gray when the final word came at five-forty A.M. Immediately, the Marine Corps launched the drive to take Kwajulane, one of the largest Japanese bases on the nearby island. Shells began raining onto the shore from the gray hulks of the battleships.

There was a faint noise in the distance, which soon built into a roar as allied dive-bombers headed toward the small island. Bombs blasted huge holes in the ground and reduced buildings to rubble. As star flares lit the still-dark sky, men poured out of the smaller boats and began splashing through the water. When the marines were sighted, bullets began raining down, killing some and injuring others. Still they pressed on.

A war correspondent came in a raft behind the first line of men and happened upon two marines that had been shot while they were still in the water. It was easy to tell that one of them was badly wounded because of the redness of the water. Another soldier who was also injured was holding the man's head above the water.

The correspondent pulled them into his boat amidst a hail of bullets from shore, then quickly moved back to a safer location in order to render first aid. The young man who had been unconscious in the water seemed too far gone to need help. Yet his friend refused to be attended to until he was looked at. Medics came, and even though they administered first aid to the severely wounded marine, they could see his condition was hopeless. They told his friend that he would be dead in a matter of minutes.

The young man, his face bronzed by the tropical sun, stared at his critically injured friend in disbelief. Then, moving slowly and carefully, so as not to disturb the injured man, the soldier got to his knees. His one arm was useless. In fact, it was nearly gone, so he used his one good arm to cautiously place the unconscious man's head on his lap. Then, placing his good hand on the other's pale forehead, he uttered words that astonished the correspondent, a blessing that the reporter later said was emblazoned in unforgettable letters across the doorway of his memory:

"In the name of Jesus Christ, and by the virtue of the Holy Priesthood which I hold, I command you to remain alive until the necessary help can be obtained to secure the preservation of your life."[1]

Heavenly Father honored the blessing the young marine gave to his friend. The rescuers managed to keep the critically injured man alive until they could get back to the ship. There, doctors worked frantically to save him. Against all odds, the critically wounded marine continued to hold onto life as the ship took the injured to a hospital in Honolulu.

After he arrived, it took some time before the doctors were able to say he would live. During his convalescence, he was the wonder of the medical unit. Everyone knew that death was a foregone conclusion for anyone with such severe injuries. How and why he had managed to live remained a deep mystery to the medical staff. But it wasn't a mystery to the faithful young marine who had been heroic enough to put aside the pain of his own wounds in order to administer to his friend.

Weeks later, the war correspondent went back to that hospital in Honolulu to visit the two young men he had helped pull into his boat. It was nothing less than a miracle, he thought, that the three of them could walk down to the beach.

As they strolled along, watching the waves roll in, they talked together and marveled at the power of God.

Notes

1. Robert B. Fox, compiler, *Courage To Live,* (Salt Lake City: Deseret Book, 1967), p. 80.

Index